D1461484

Rupert Fawcett's brilliantly observed Off The Leash
cartoons about dogs have a huge global following.
With *On The Prowl* he brings his trademark wit
and warmth to the world of cats.

The Secret Life of Cats is a celebration of our
furry feline friends in all their paw-licking, foot-clawing,
sofa-hogging glory. Featuring their secret thoughts and
conversations, it will make anyone who has ever
owned a cat laugh out loud in recognition.

Also by Rupert Fawcett

Off The Leash: The Secret Life of Dogs
Off The Leash: A Dog's Best Friend
Off The Leash: It's a Dog's Life

On The Prowl

THE SECRET LIFE OF CATS

Rupert Fawcett

BOXTREE

First published in 2016 by Boxtree
an imprint of Pan Macmillan
20 New Wharf Road, London N1 9RR
Associated companies throughout the world
www.panmacmillan.com

ISBN 978-0-7522-6615-2

1 3 5 7 9 8 6 4 2

A CIP catalogue record for this book is available from the British Library.

Printed and bound in Italy by Rotolito Lombarda.

Visit **www.panmacmillan.com** to read more about all our books
and to buy them. You will also find features, author interviews and
news of any author events, and you can sign up for e-newsletters
so that you're always first to hear about our new releases.

Foreword

It's impossible for a cartoonist like me to live with two cats and not keep coming up with ideas for cat cartoons. Cats are so inscrutable and funny that I just couldn't resist trying to immortalize their adorable weirdness in pen and ink.

Having had three *Off The Leash* books published all around the world, it has been great fun to turn my attention from canines to felines, and the response from my On The Prowl Facebook followers has inspired me to keep going and create this collection.

Whether you are a cat owner, a former cat owner or neither, I hope you will find something in this book that will make you purr.

Rupert Fawcett

For cat lovers everywhere

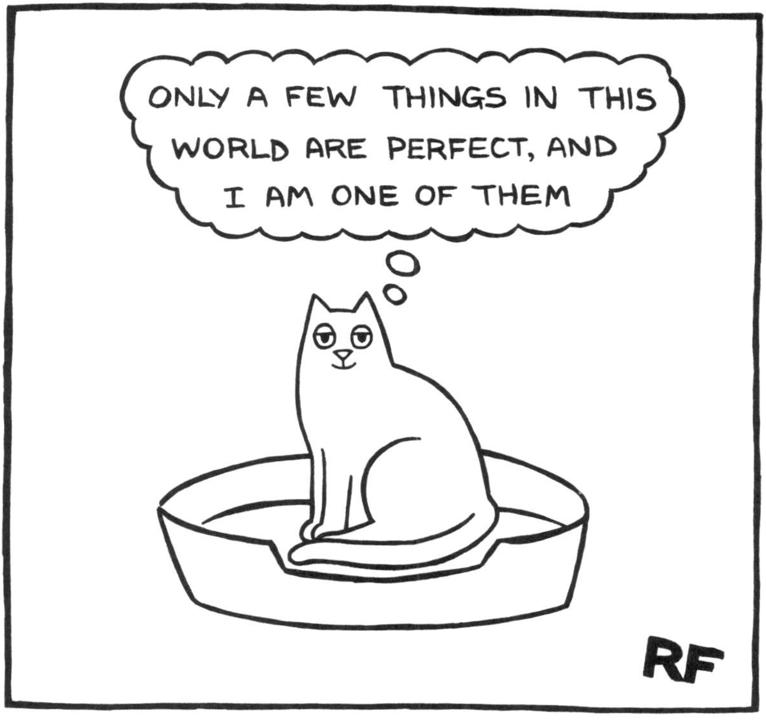
ONLY A FEW THINGS IN THIS WORLD ARE PERFECT, AND I AM ONE OF THEM
RF

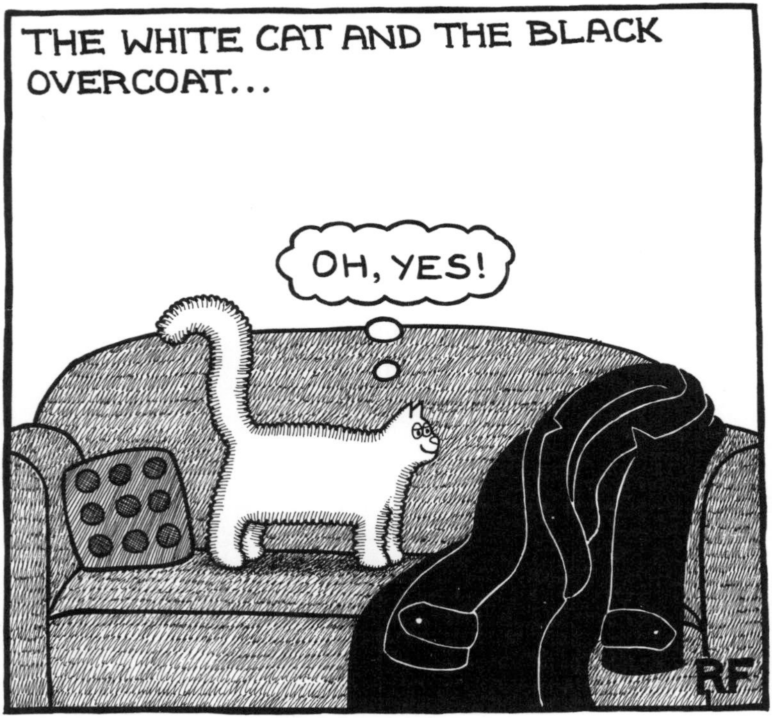
THE WHITE CAT AND THE BLACK OVERCOAT...
OH, YES!
RF

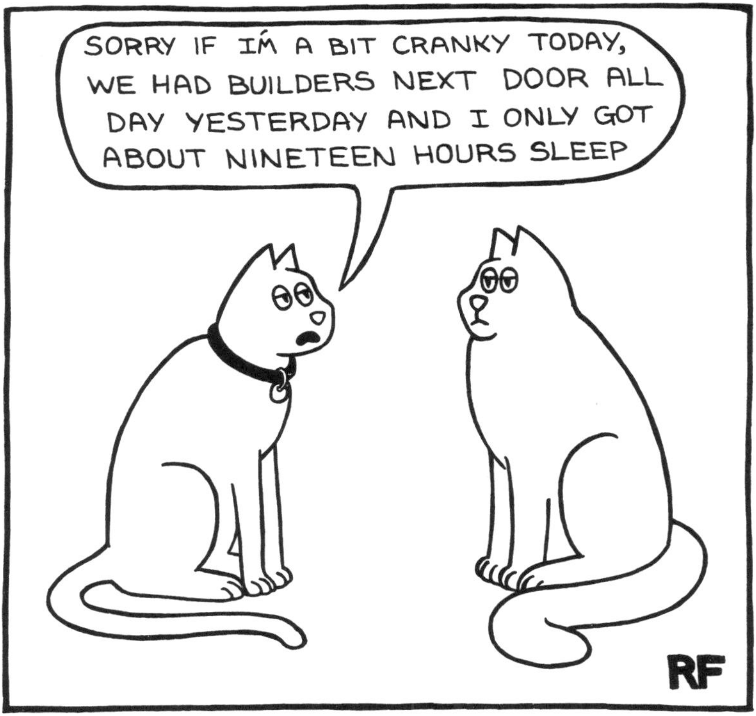
SORRY IF I'M A BIT CRANKY TODAY, WE HAD BUILDERS NEXT DOOR ALL DAY YESTERDAY AND I ONLY GOT ABOUT NINETEEN HOURS SLEEP
RF

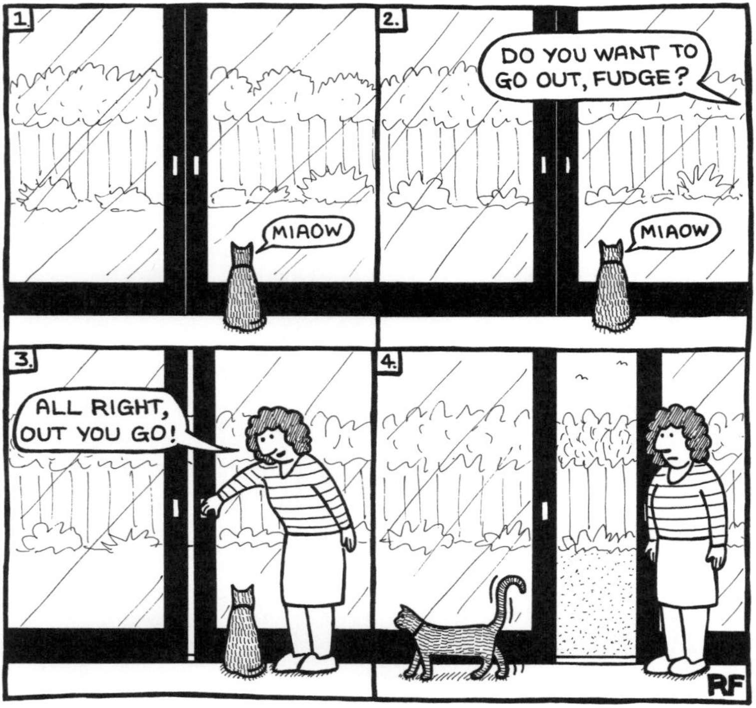
1.
MIAOW
2.
DO YOU WANT TO GO OUT, FUDGE?
MIAOW
3.
ALL RIGHT, OUT YOU GO!
4.
RF

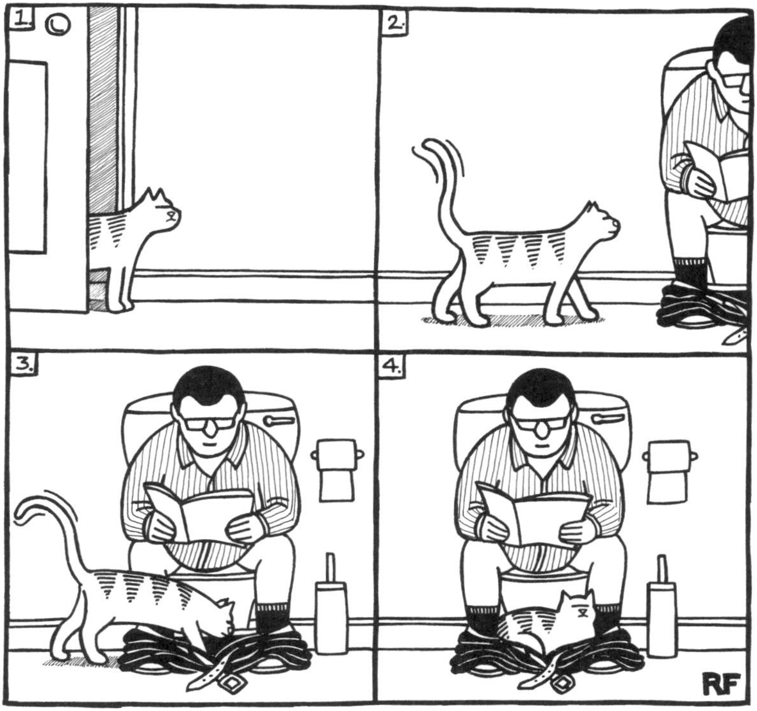
1.
2.
3.
4.
RF

THE BELLY-SCRATCH FLIP...

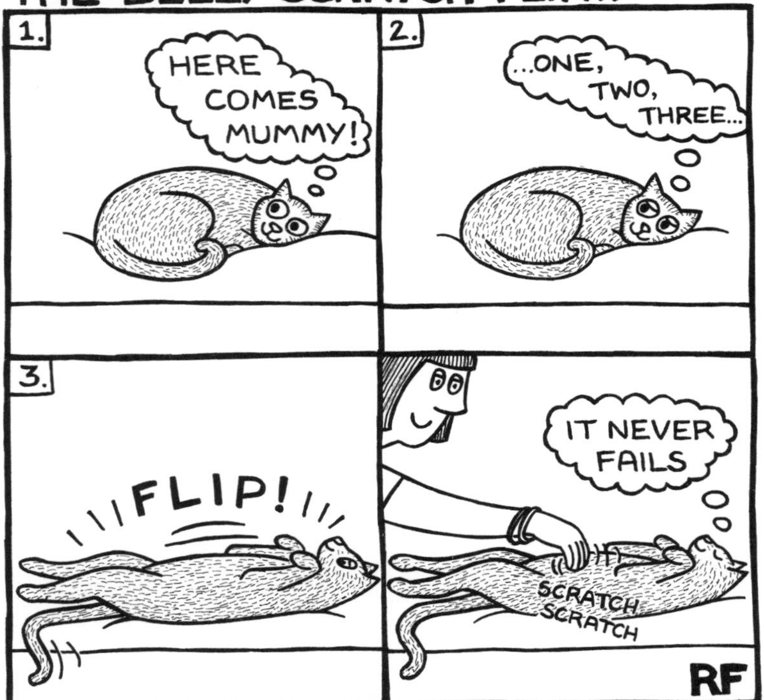

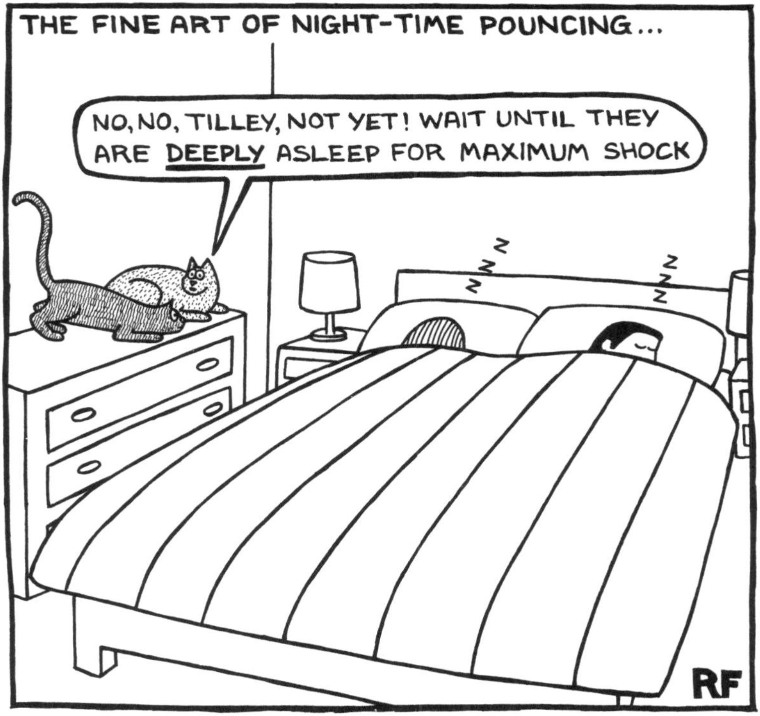
THE FINE ART OF NIGHT-TIME POUNCING...
NO, NO, TILLEY, NOT YET! WAIT UNTIL THEY ARE DEEPLY ASLEEP FOR MAXIMUM SHOCK
Z Z Z
Z Z Z
RF

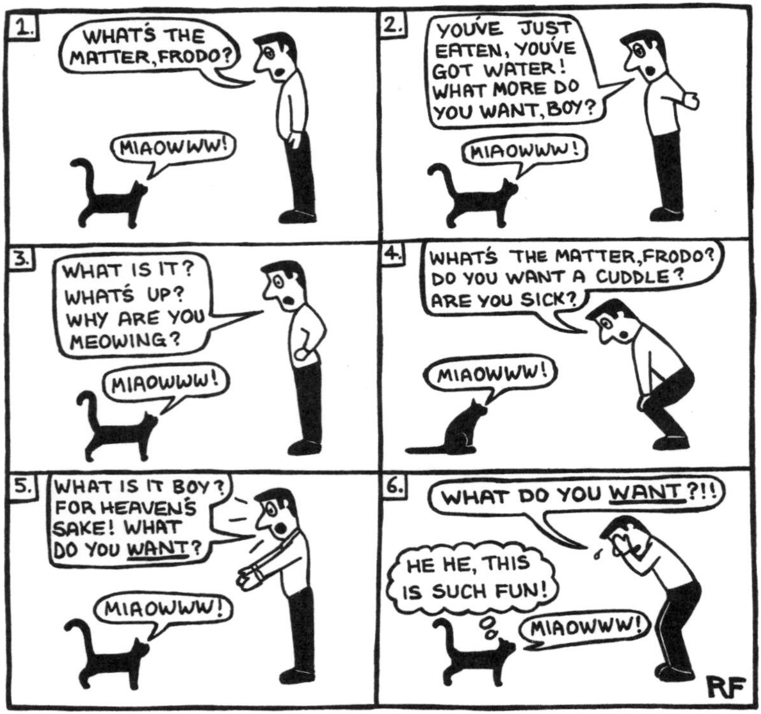
1.
WHAT'S THE MATTER, FRODO?
MIAOWWW!
2.
YOU'VE JUST EATEN, YOU'VE GOT WATER! WHAT MORE DO YOU WANT, BOY?
MIAOWWW!
3.
WHAT IS IT? WHAT'S UP? WHY ARE YOU MEOWING?
MIAOWWW!
4.
WHAT'S THE MATTER, FRODO? DO YOU WANT A CUDDLE? ARE YOU SICK?
MIAOWWW!
5.
WHAT IS IT BOY? FOR HEAVEN'S SAKE! WHAT DO YOU WANT?
MIAOWWW!
6.
WHAT DO YOU WANT?!!
HE HE, THIS IS SUCH FUN!
MIAOWWW!
RF

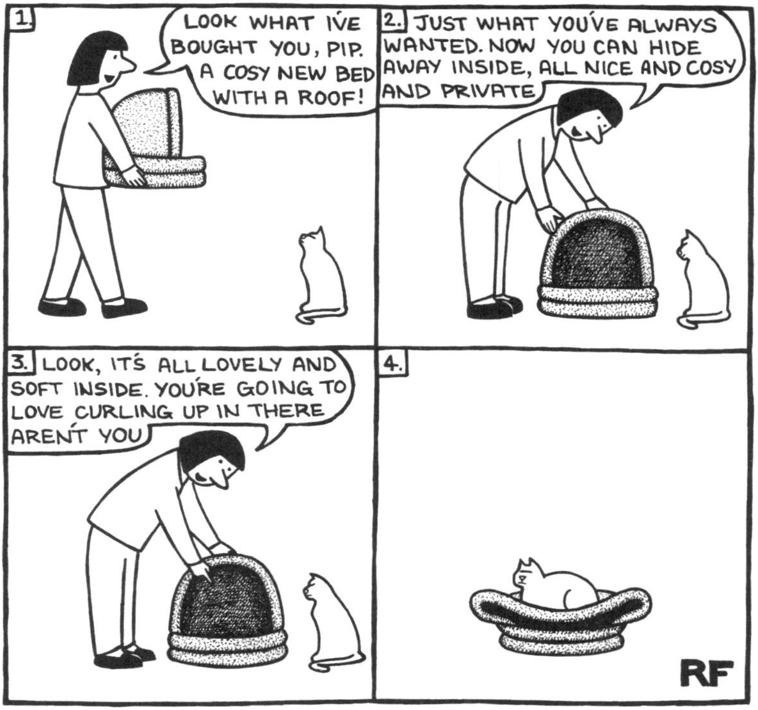
1.
LOOK WHAT I'VE BOUGHT YOU, PIP. A COSY NEW BED WITH A ROOF!
2.
JUST WHAT YOU'VE ALWAYS WANTED. NOW YOU CAN HIDE AWAY INSIDE, ALL NICE AND COSY AND PRIVATE
3.
LOOK, IT'S ALL LOVELY AND SOFT INSIDE. YOU'RE GOING TO LOVE CURLING UP IN THERE AREN'T YOU
4.
RF

THE BATHTIME ROUTINE...

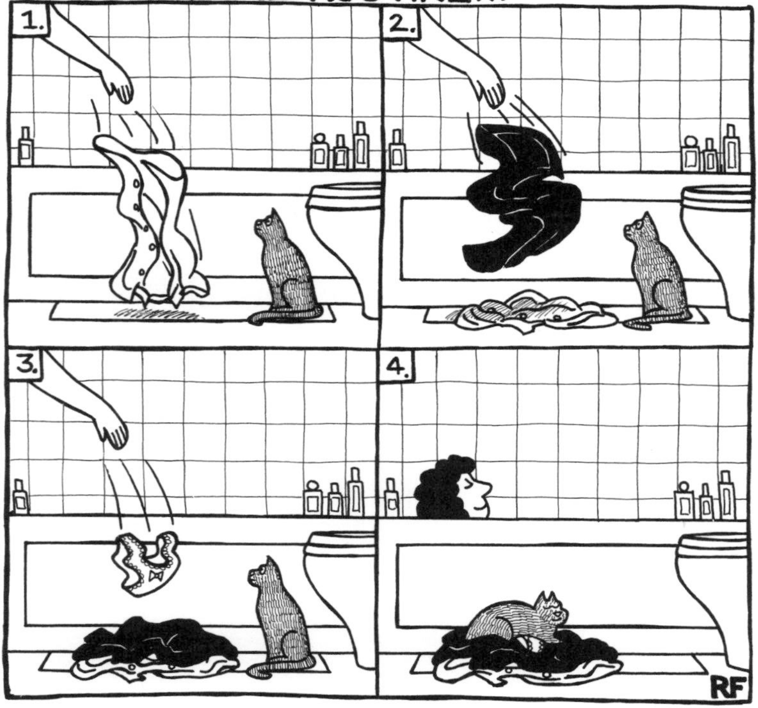
1.
2.
3.
4.
RF

A DIFFERENCE OF OPINION…

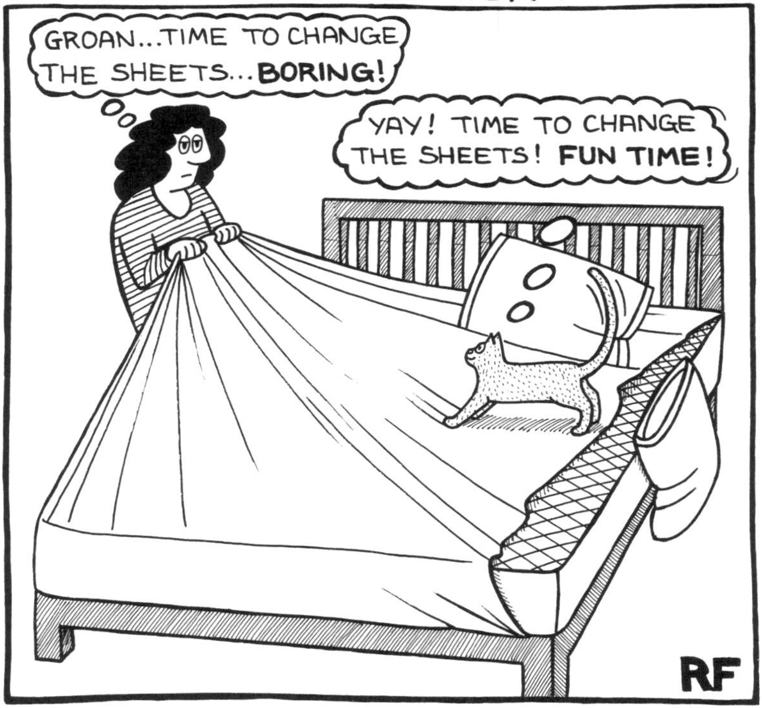
GROAN…TIME TO CHANGE THE SHEETS…**BORING!**
YAY! TIME TO CHANGE THE SHEETS! **FUN TIME!**
RF

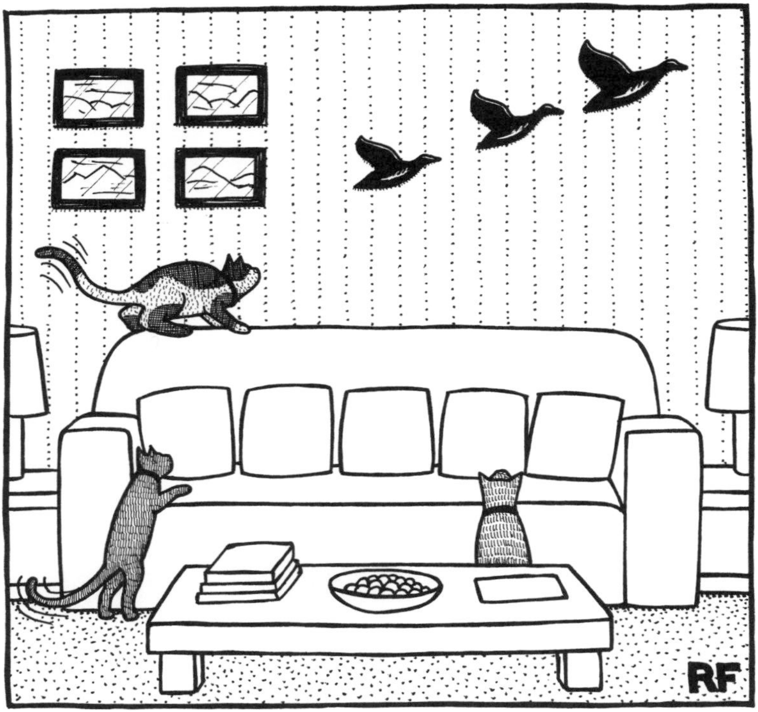
RF

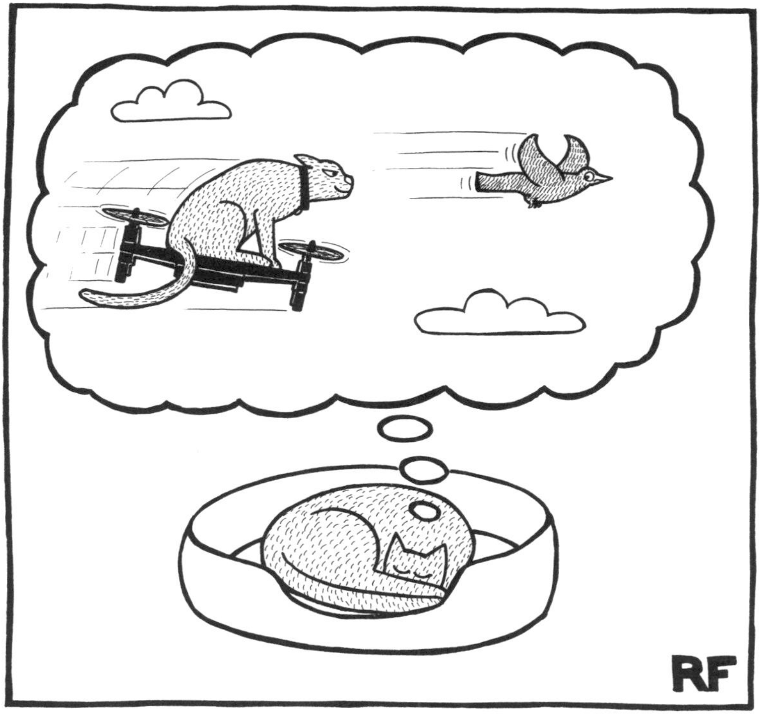
RF

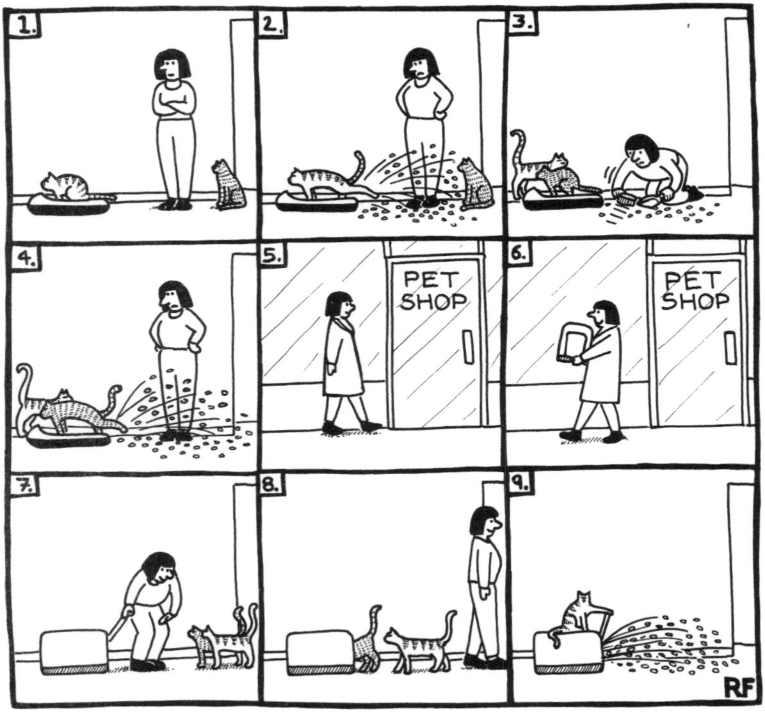
1.
2.
3.
4.
5.
PET SHOP
6.
PET SHOP
7.
8.
9.
RF

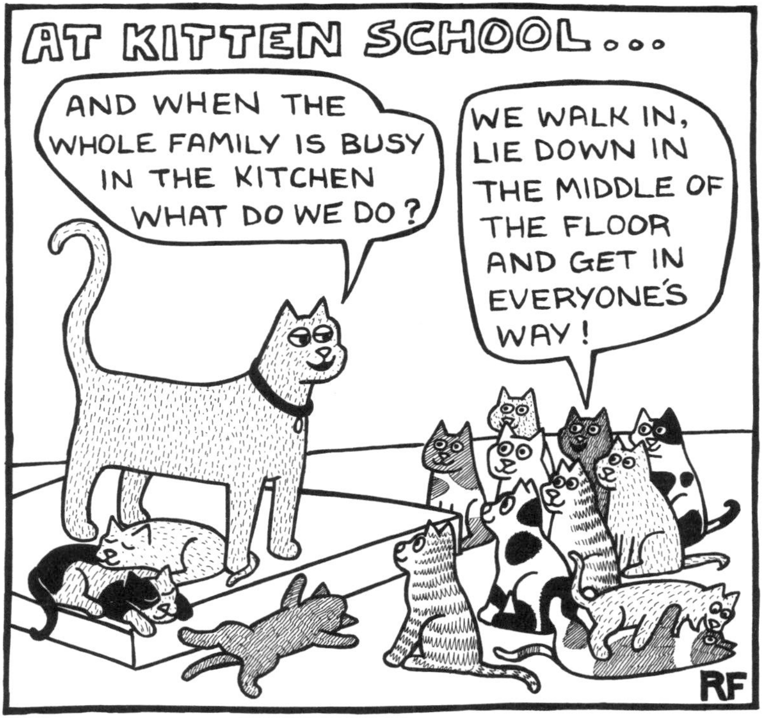
AT KITTEN SCHOOL...
AND WHEN THE WHOLE FAMILY IS BUSY IN THE KITCHEN WHAT DO WE DO?
WE WALK IN, LIE DOWN IN THE MIDDLE OF THE FLOOR AND GET IN EVERYONE'S WAY!
RF

UNDERSTANDING DOGS AND THEIR OWNERS...

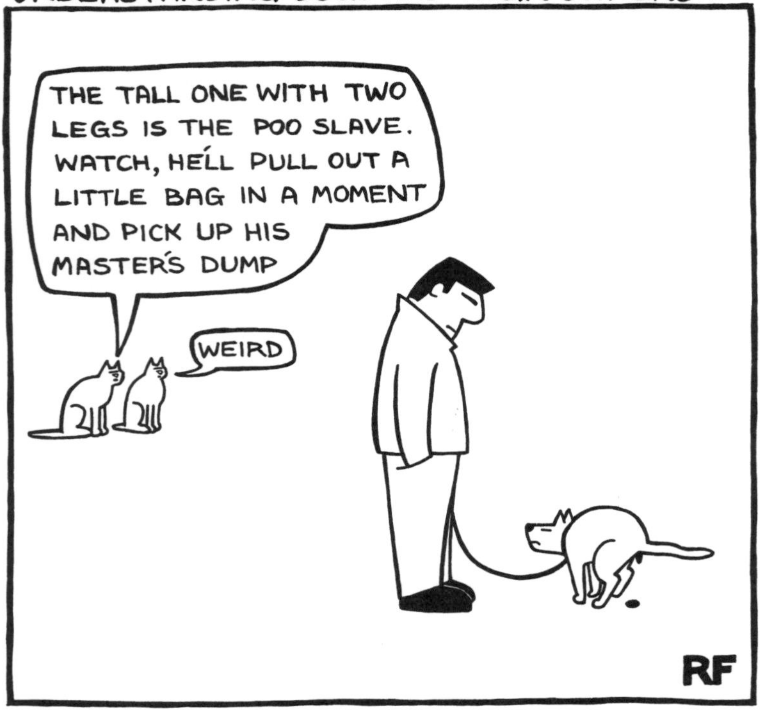

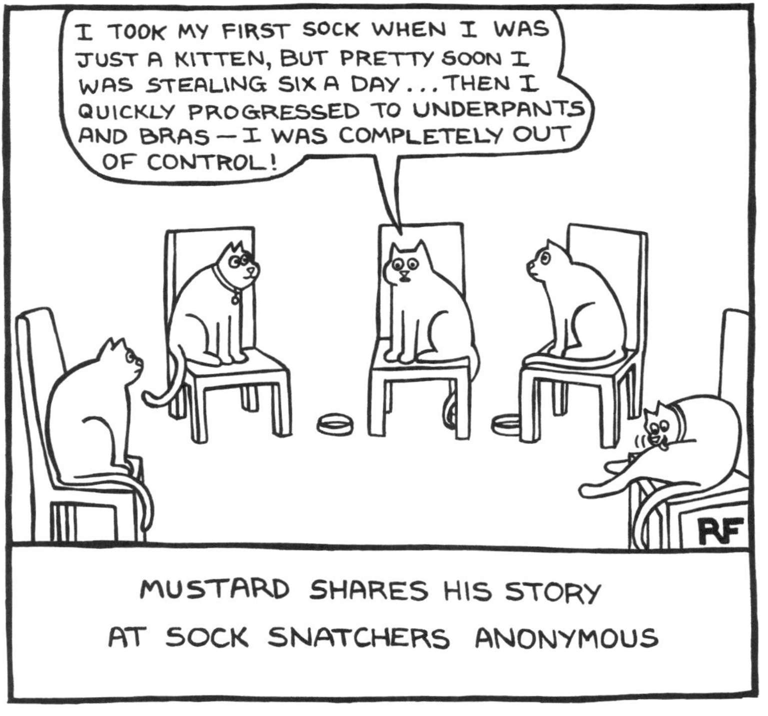
I TOOK MY FIRST SOCK WHEN I WAS JUST A KITTEN, BUT PRETTY SOON I WAS STEALING SIX A DAY . . . THEN I QUICKLY PROGRESSED TO UNDERPANTS AND BRAS — I WAS COMPLETELY OUT OF CONTROL!
RF

MUSTARD SHARES HIS STORY AT SOCK SNATCHERS ANONYMOUS

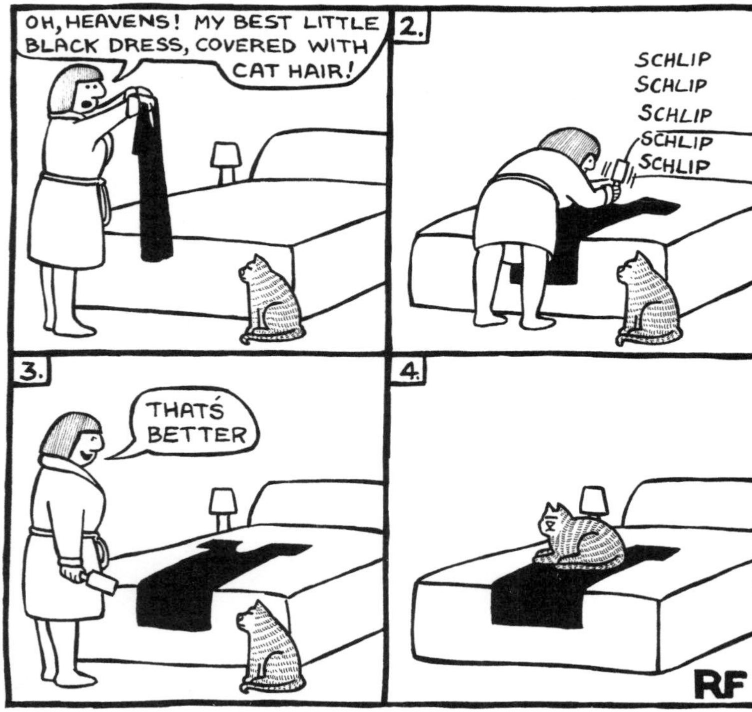
OH, HEAVENS! MY BEST LITTLE BLACK DRESS, COVERED WITH CAT HAIR!
2.
SCHLIP
SCHLIP
SCHLIP
SCHLIP
SCHLIP
3.
THATŚ BETTER
4.
RF

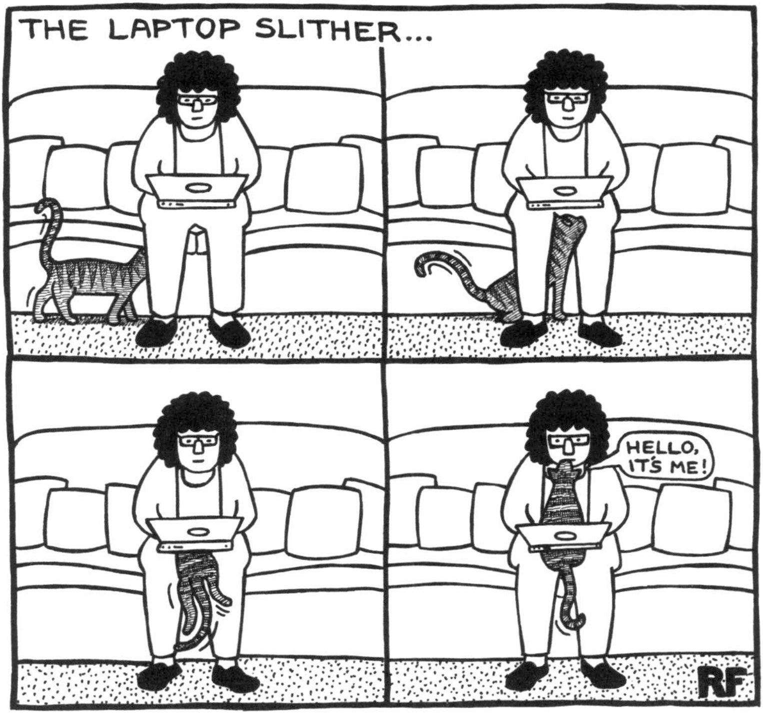
THE LAPTOP SLITHER...
HELLO, IT'S ME!
RF

AT KITTEN HIGH SCHOOL...

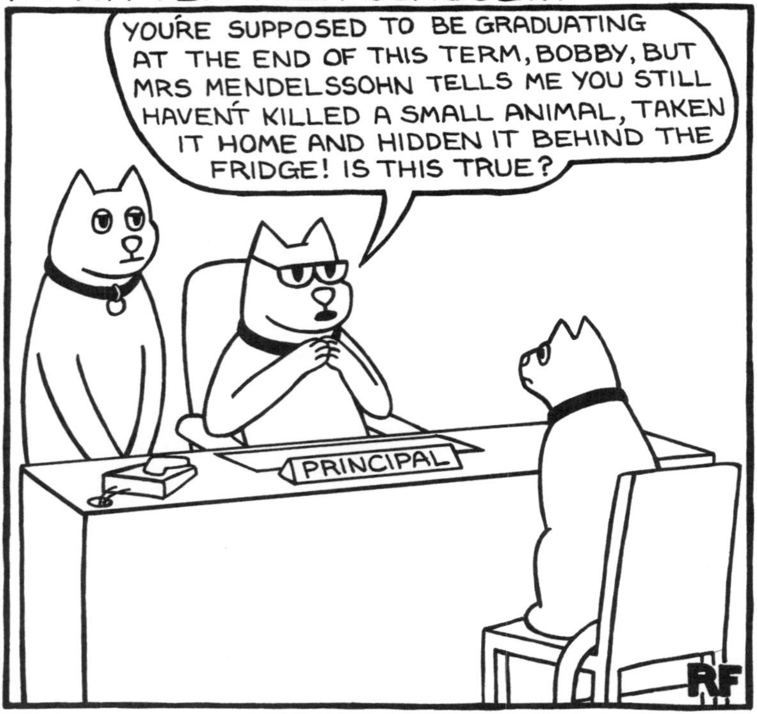
YOU'RE SUPPOSED TO BE GRADUATING AT THE END OF THIS TERM, BOBBY, BUT MRS MENDELSSOHN TELLS ME YOU STILL HAVEN'T KILLED A SMALL ANIMAL, TAKEN IT HOME AND HIDDEN IT BEHIND THE FRIDGE! IS THIS TRUE?
PRINCIPAL
RF

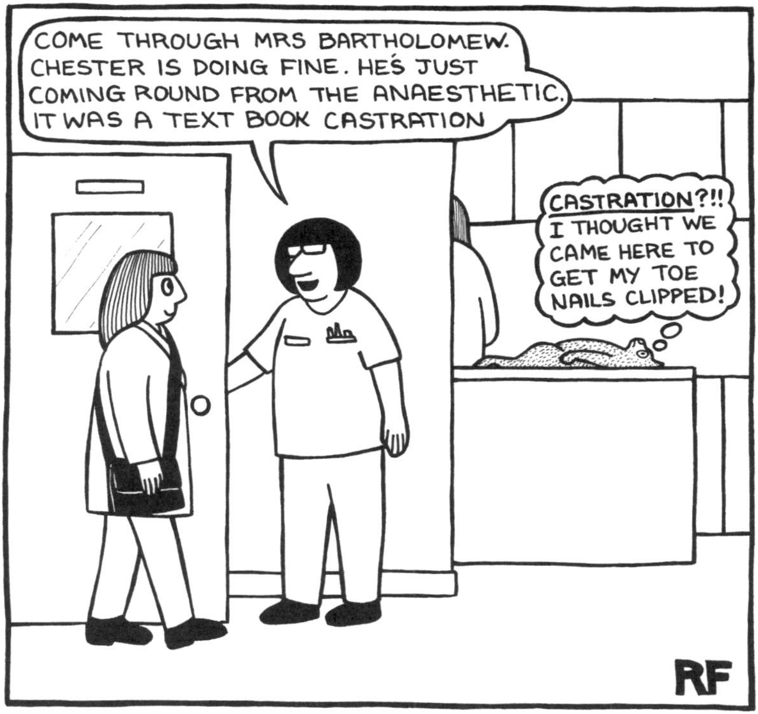
COME THROUGH MRS BARTHOLOMEW. CHESTER IS DOING FINE. HE'S JUST COMING ROUND FROM THE ANAESTHETIC. IT WAS A TEXT BOOK CASTRATION
CASTRATION?!! I THOUGHT WE CAME HERE TO GET MY TOE NAILS CLIPPED!
RF

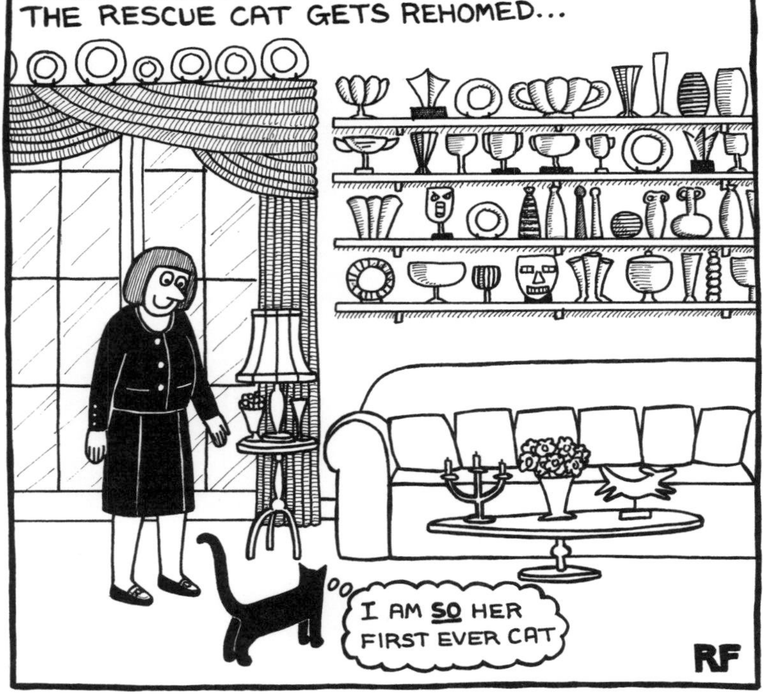
THE RESCUE CAT GETS REHOMED...
I AM SO HER FIRST EVER CAT
RF

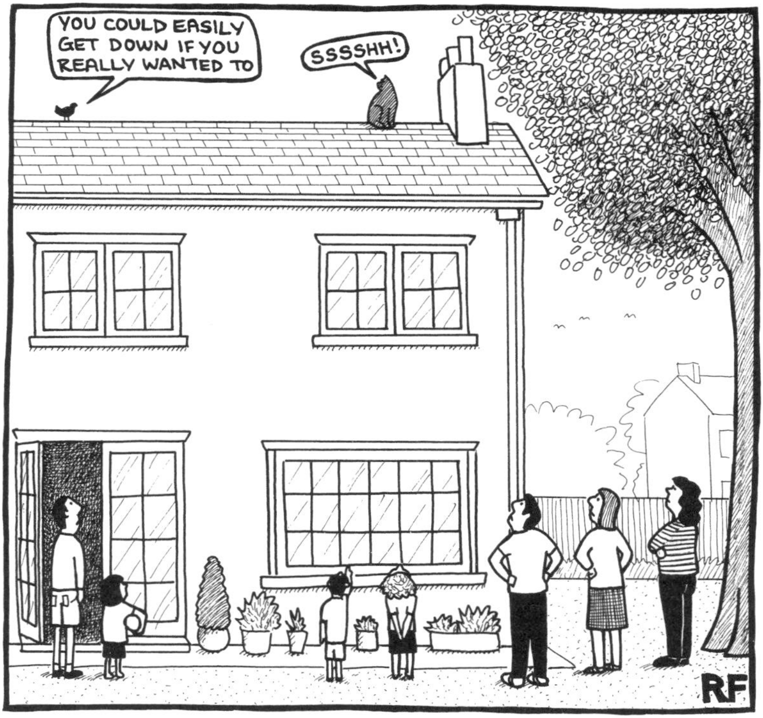
YOU COULD EASILY GET DOWN IF YOU REALLY WANTED TO
SSSSHH!
RF

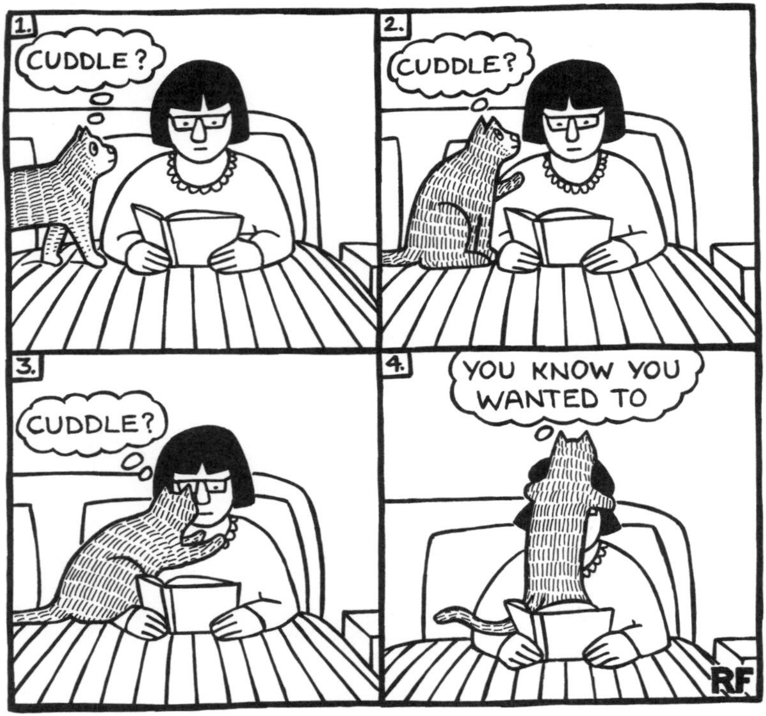
1.
CUDDLE?
2.
CUDDLE?
3.
CUDDLE?
4.
YOU KNOW YOU WANTED TO
RF

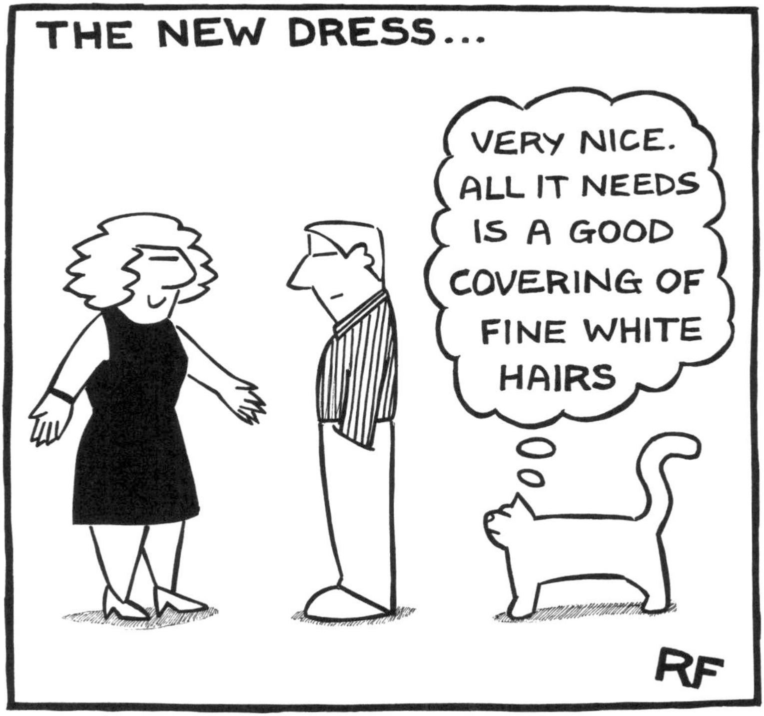
THE NEW DRESS...
VERY NICE. ALL IT NEEDS IS A GOOD COVERING OF FINE WHITE HAIRS
RF

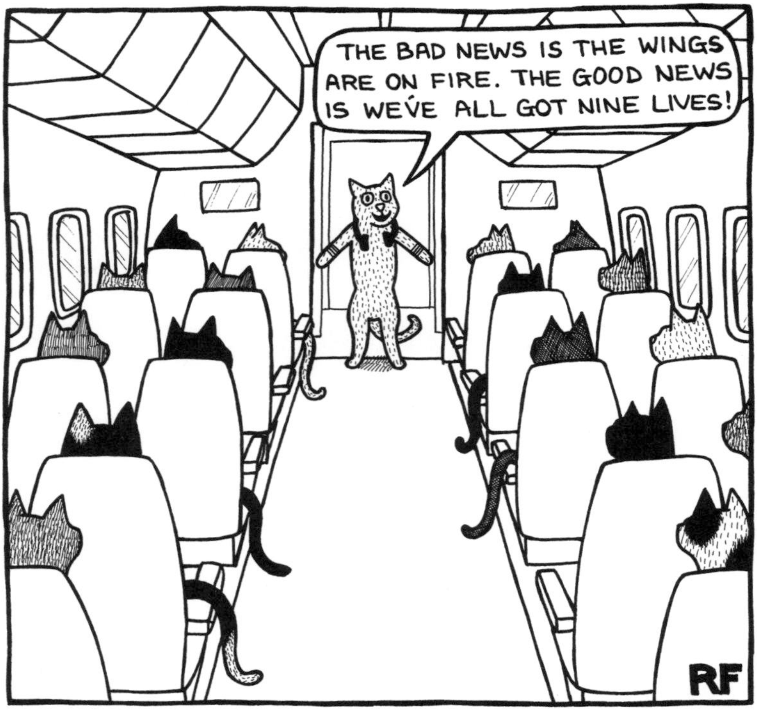
THE BAD NEWS IS THE WINGS ARE ON FIRE. THE GOOD NEWS IS WE'VE ALL GOT NINE LIVES!
RF

FOUR POSITIONS OF A GUARD CAT...

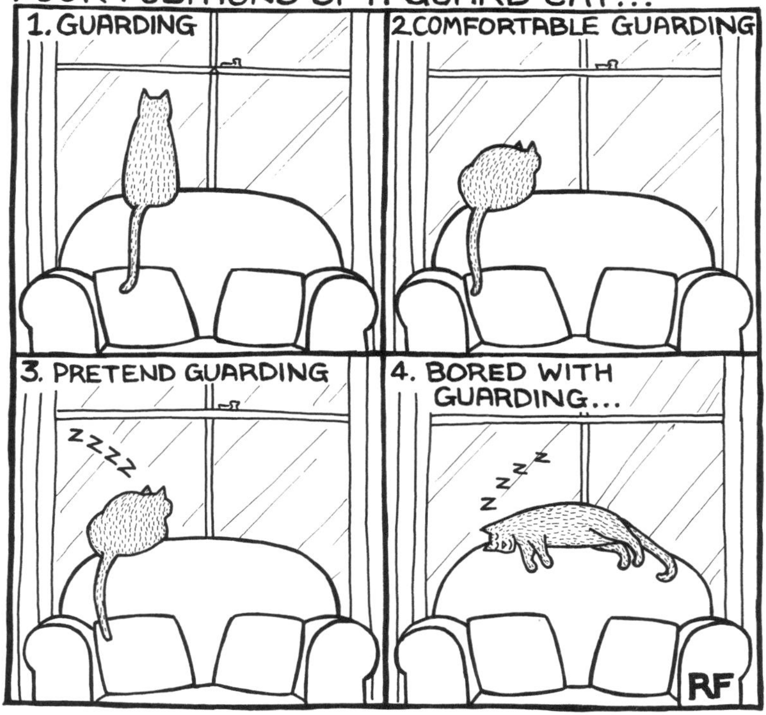
1. GUARDING
2. COMFORTABLE GUARDING
3. PRETEND GUARDING
ZZZZ
4. BORED WITH GUARDING...
ZZZZ
RF

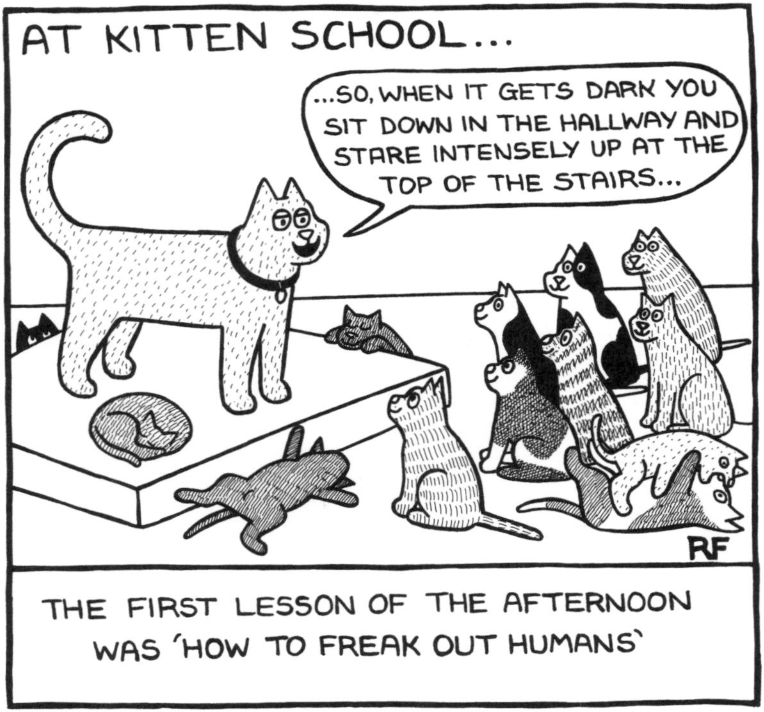
AT KITTEN SCHOOL...
...SO, WHEN IT GETS DARK YOU SIT DOWN IN THE HALLWAY AND STARE INTENSELY UP AT THE TOP OF THE STAIRS...
RF
THE FIRST LESSON OF THE AFTERNOON WAS 'HOW TO FREAK OUT HUMANS'

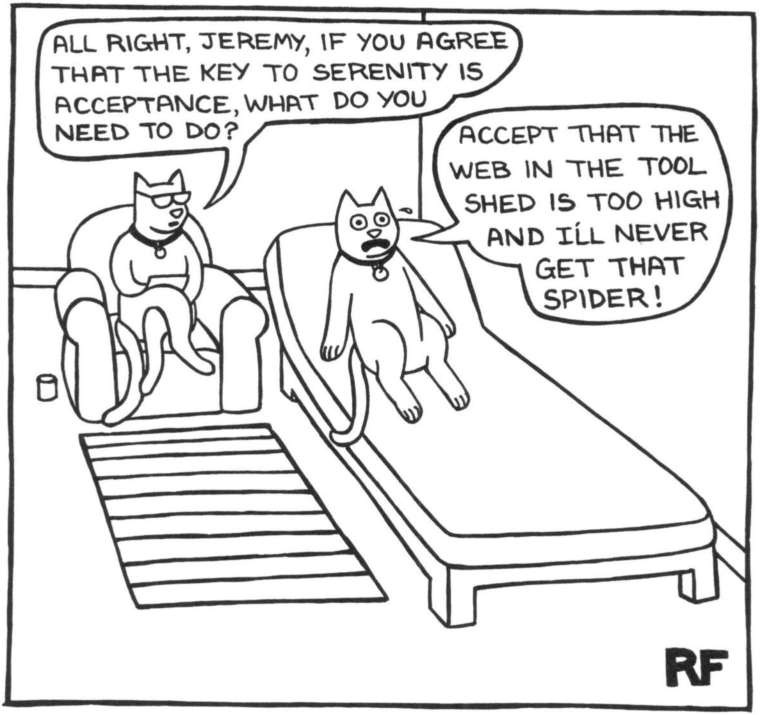
ALL RIGHT, JEREMY, IF YOU AGREE THAT THE KEY TO SERENITY IS ACCEPTANCE, WHAT DO YOU NEED TO DO?
ACCEPT THAT THE WEB IN THE TOOL SHED IS TOO HIGH AND I'LL NEVER GET THAT SPIDER!
RF

AT THE OSTEOPATH...
YEP, YOUR NECK HAS TOTALLY LOCKED UP, WENDY. I'VE TOLD YOU BEFORE, YOU'VE GOT TO STOP STARING UP AT THE BIRDS ON THAT T.V. AERIAL
RF

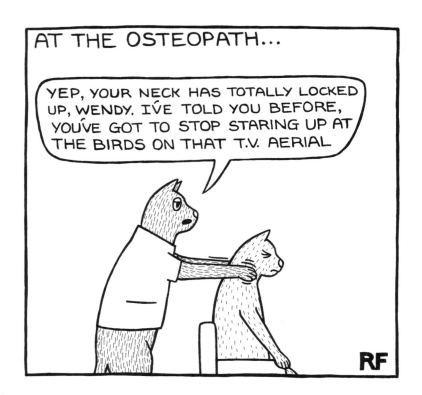

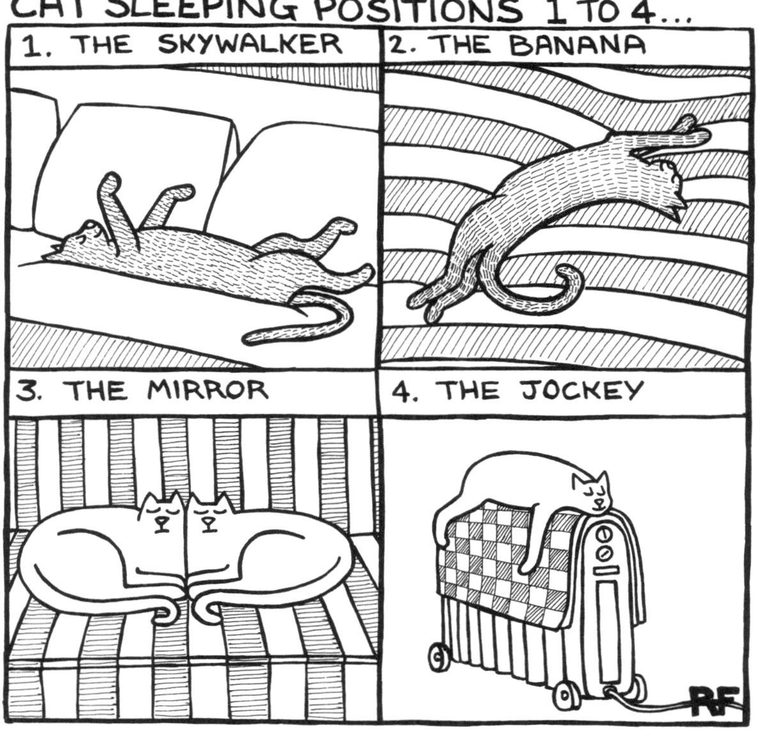
CAT SLEEPING POSITIONS 1 TO 4...
1. THE SKYWALKER
2. THE BANANA
3. THE MIRROR
4. THE JOCKEY
RF

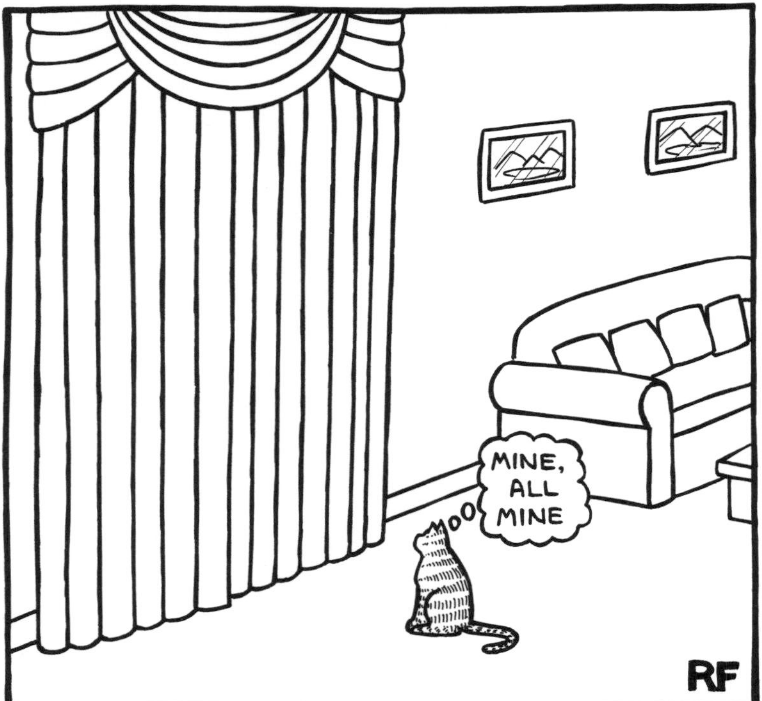
MINE, ALL MINE
MOO
RF

THE HUNT...

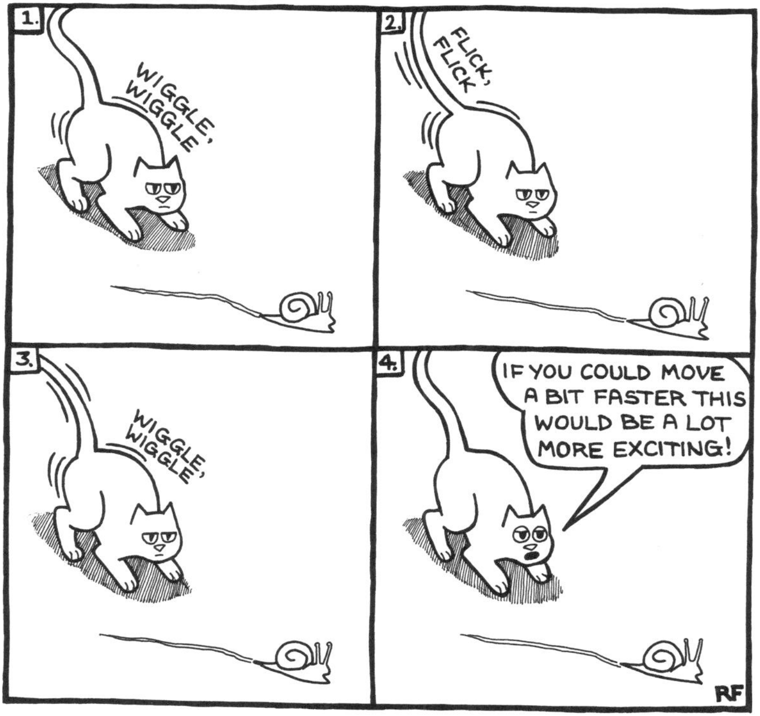
1.
WIGGLE, WIGGLE
2.
FLICK, FLICK
3.
WIGGLE, WIGGLE
4.
IF YOU COULD MOVE A BIT FASTER THIS WOULD BE A LOT MORE EXCITING!
RF

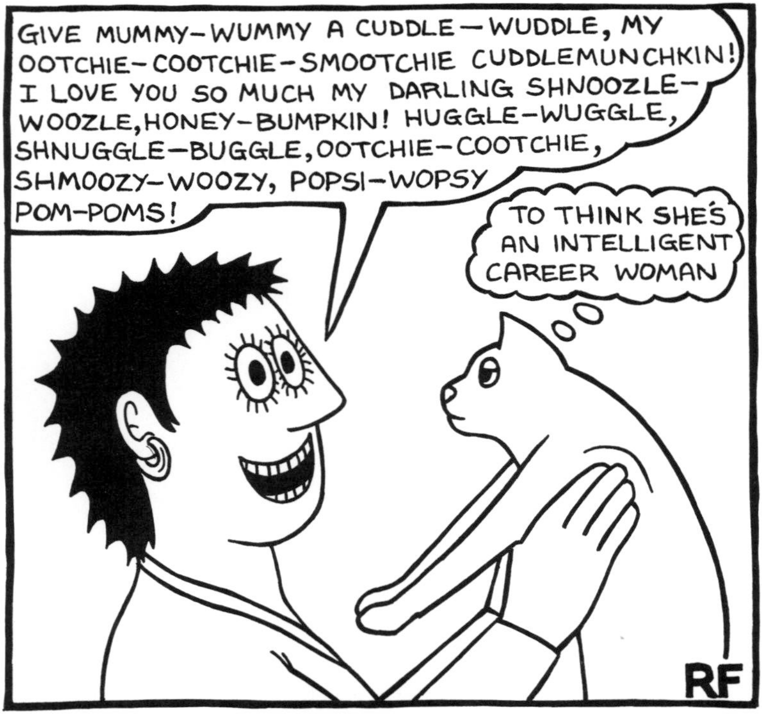
GIVE MUMMY-WUMMY A CUDDLE-WUDDLE, MY OOTCHIE-COOTCHIE-SMOOTCHIE CUDDLEMUNCHKIN! I LOVE YOU SO MUCH MY DARLING SHNOOZLE-WOOZLE, HONEY-BUMPKIN! HUGGLE-WUGGLE, SHNUGGLE-BUGGLE, OOTCHIE-COOTCHIE, SHMOOZY-WOOZY, POPSI-WOPSY POM-POMS!
TO THINK SHE'S AN INTELLIGENT CAREER WOMAN
RF

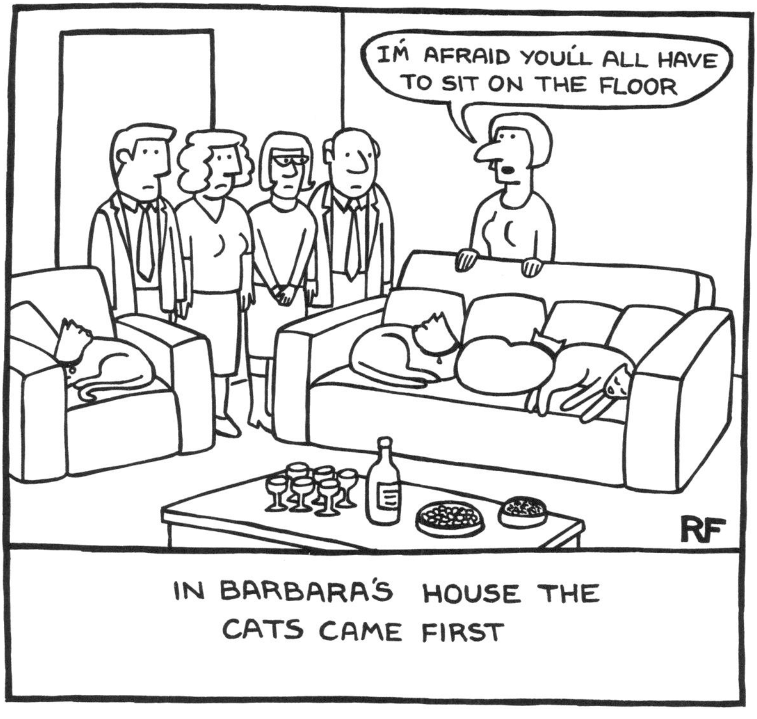
IM AFRAID YOULL ALL HAVE TO SIT ON THE FLOOR
RF

IN BARBARA'S HOUSE THE CATS CAME FIRST

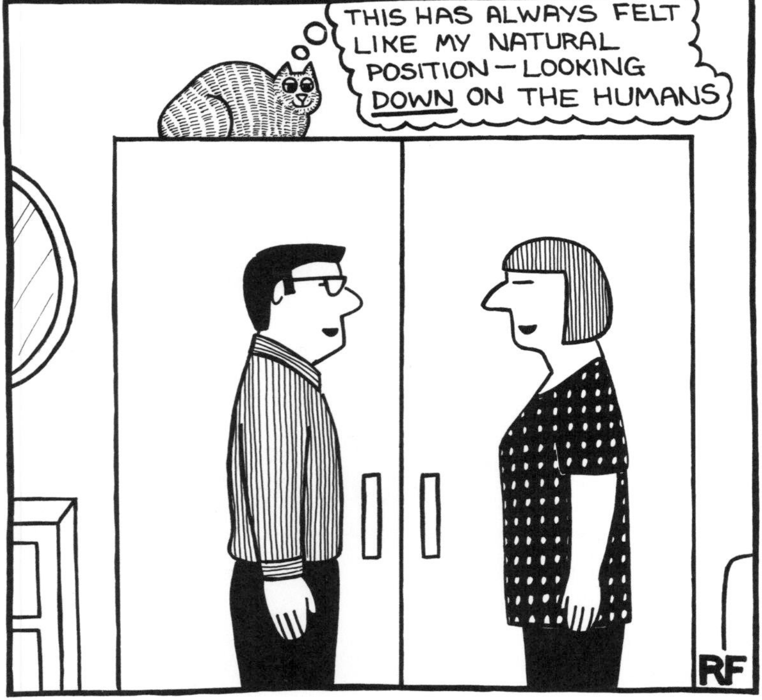
THIS HAS ALWAYS FELT LIKE MY NATURAL POSITION – LOOKING DOWN ON THE HUMANS
RF

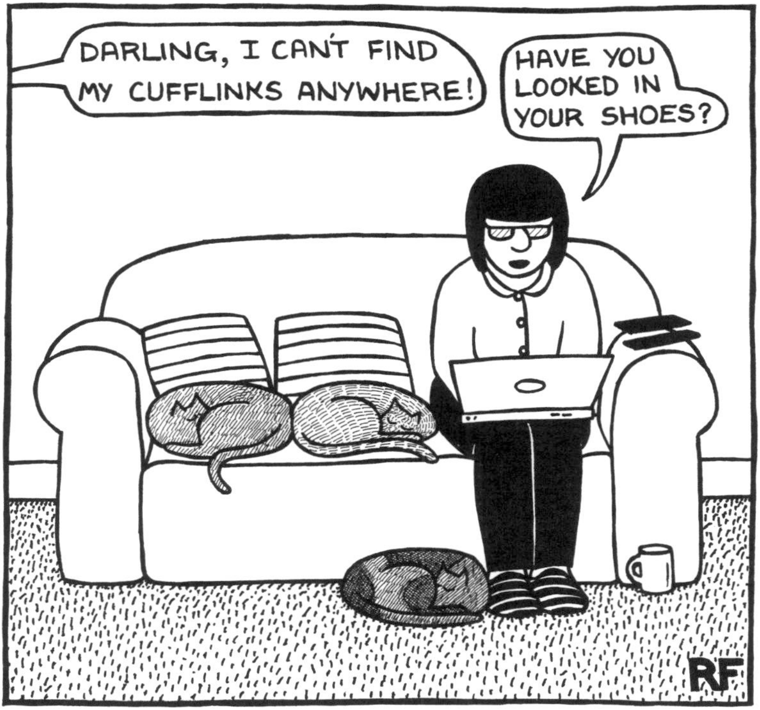
DARLING, I CAN'T FIND MY CUFFLINKS ANYWHERE!
HAVE YOU LOOKED IN YOUR SHOES?
RF

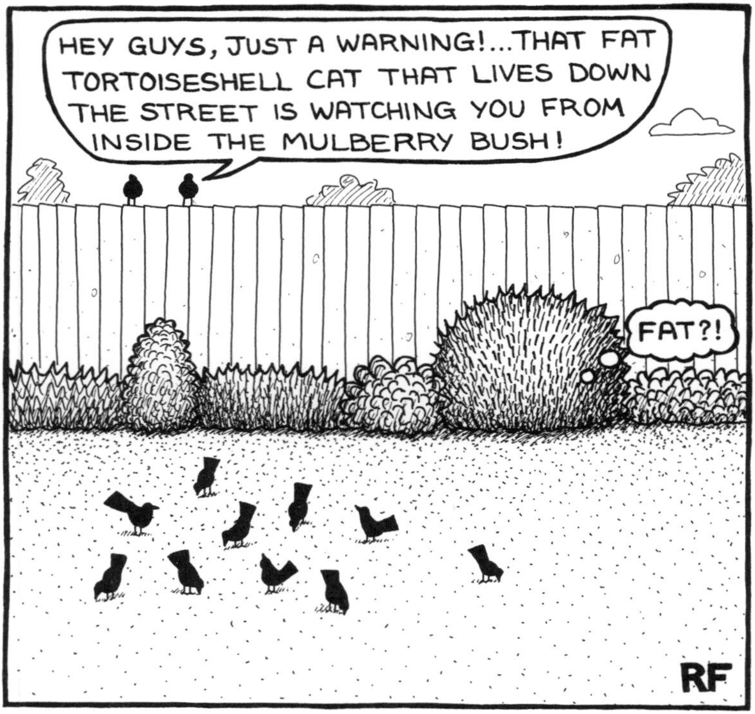
HEY GUYS, JUST A WARNING!...THAT FAT TORTOISESHELL CAT THAT LIVES DOWN THE STREET IS WATCHING YOU FROM INSIDE THE MULBERRY BUSH!
FAT?!
RF

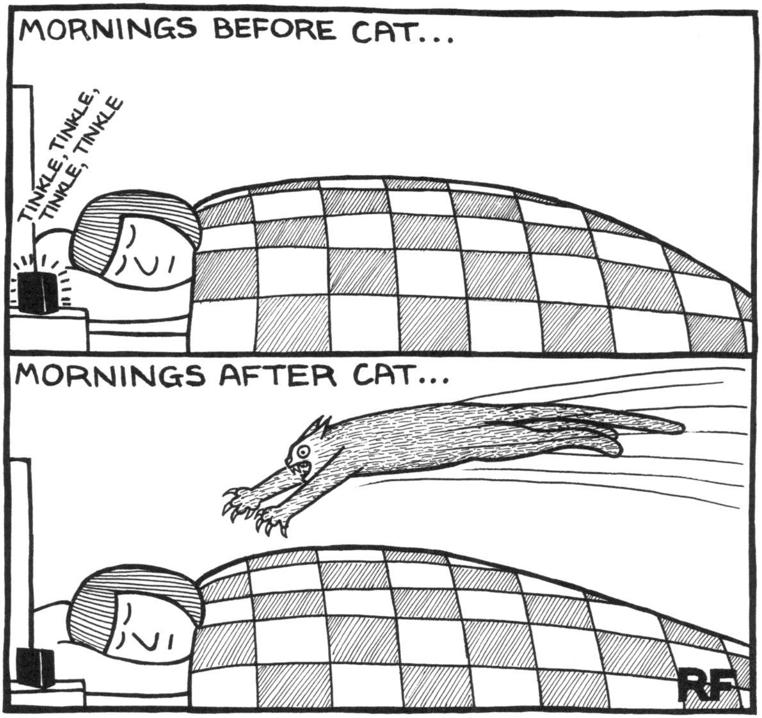
MORNINGS BEFORE CAT...
TINKLE, TINKLE, TINKLE, TINKLE
MORNINGS AFTER CAT...
RF

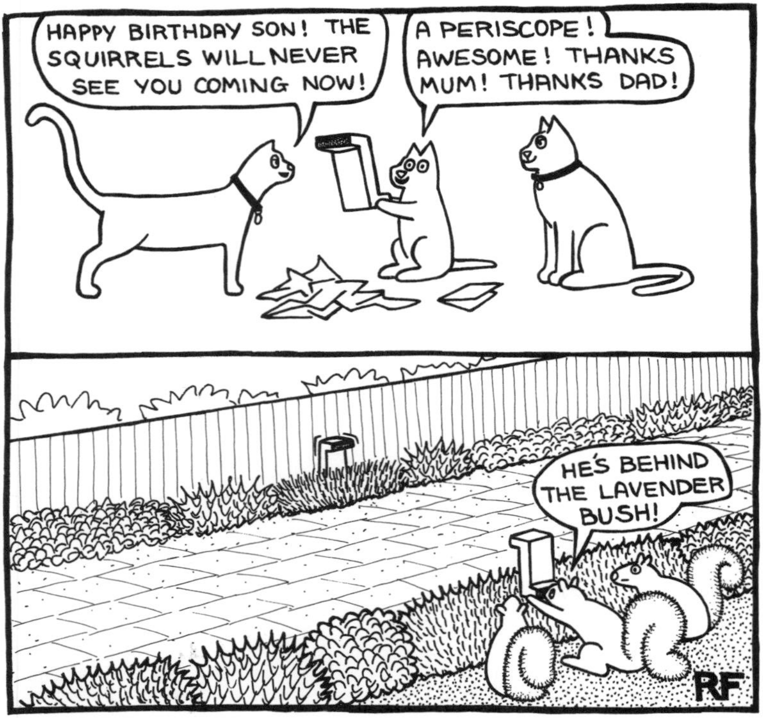
HAPPY BIRTHDAY SON! THE SQUIRRELS WILL NEVER SEE YOU COMING NOW!
A PERISCOPE! AWESOME! THANKS MUM! THANKS DAD!
HE'S BEHIND THE LAVENDER BUSH!
RF

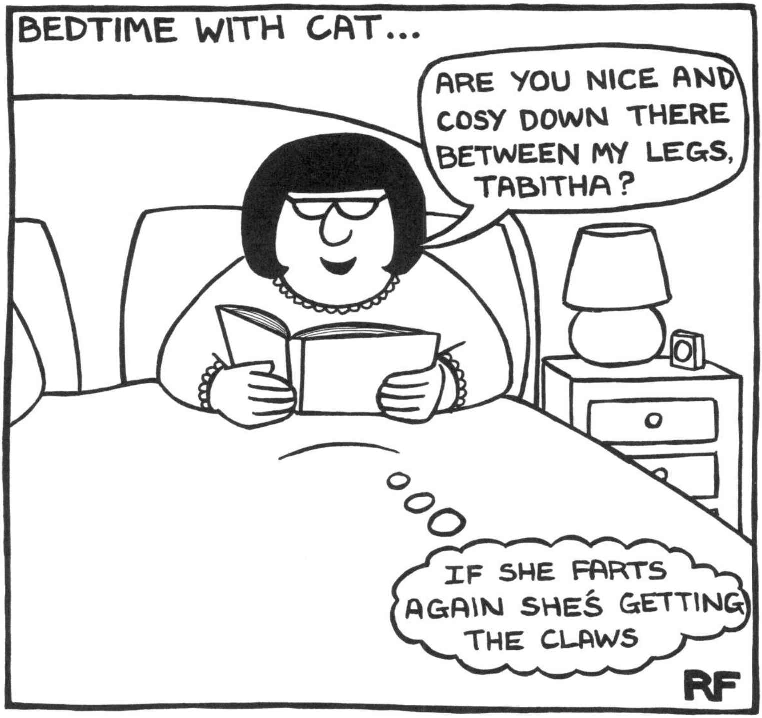
BEDTIME WITH CAT...
ARE YOU NICE AND COSY DOWN THERE BETWEEN MY LEGS, TABITHA?
IF SHE FARTS AGAIN SHE'S GETTING THE CLAWS
RF

OBJECTS OF CAT FASCINATION...

1. A BIT OF FABRIC STICKING OUT OF A DRAWER

2. TAPS

3. A SCREWED UP RECEIPT

4. A NAIL IN A WALL

RF

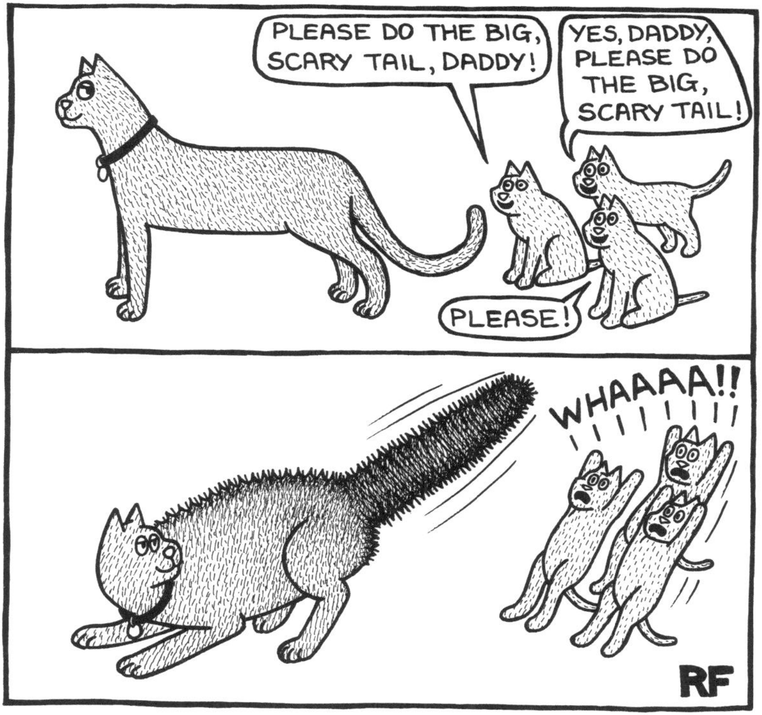
PLEASE DO THE BIG, SCARY TAIL, DADDY!
YES, DADDY, PLEASE DO THE BIG, SCARY TAIL!
PLEASE!
WHAAAAA!!
RF

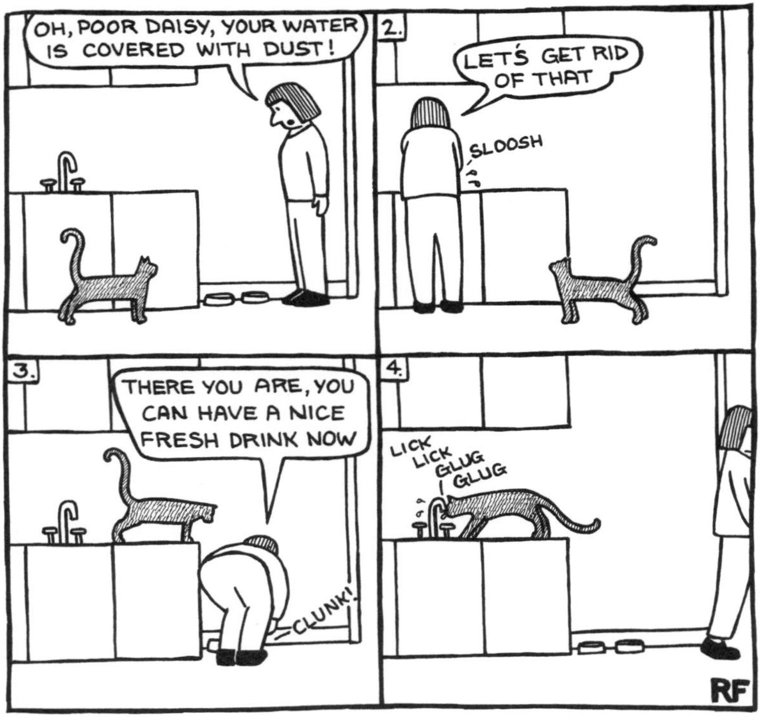
OH, POOR DAISY, YOUR WATER IS COVERED WITH DUST!
2.
LET'S GET RID OF THAT
SLOOSH
3.
THERE YOU ARE, YOU CAN HAVE A NICE FRESH DRINK NOW
CLUNK!
4.
LICK LICK GLUG GLUG
RF

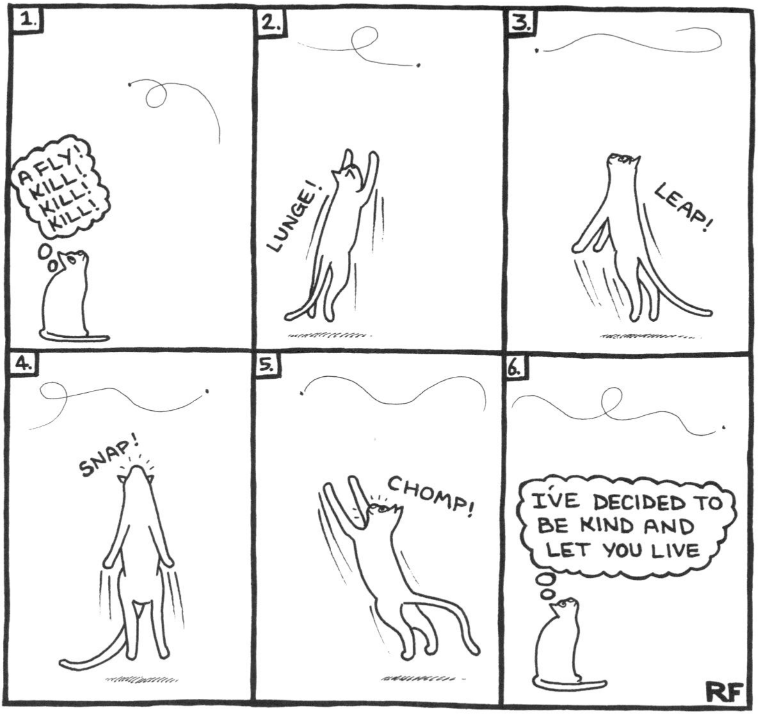
1.
A FLY! KILL! KILL! KILL!
2.
LUNGE!
3.
LEAP!
4.
SNAP!
5.
CHOMP!
6.
I'VE DECIDED TO BE KIND AND LET YOU LIVE
RF

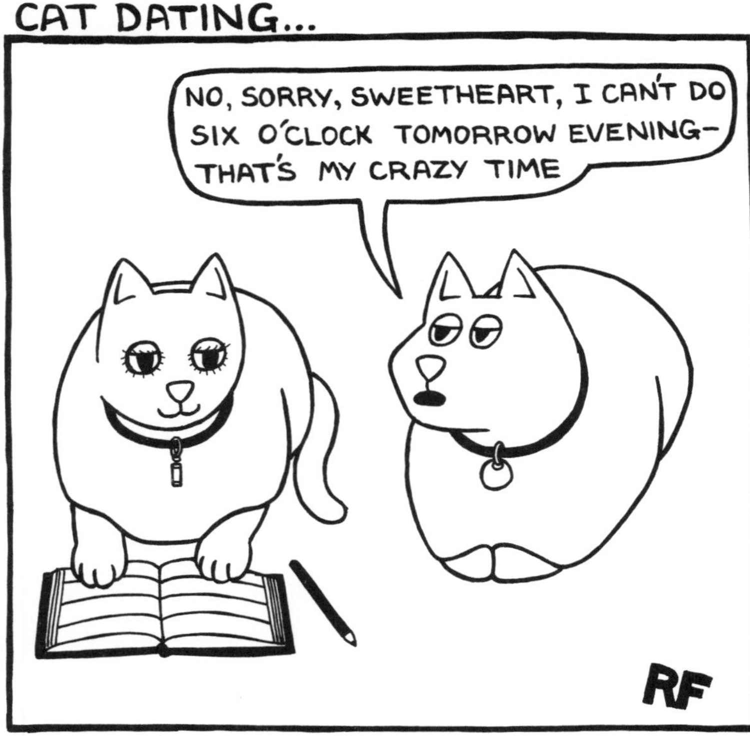
CAT DATING...
NO, SORRY, SWEETHEART, I CAN'T DO SIX O'CLOCK TOMORROW EVENING– THAT'S MY CRAZY TIME
RF

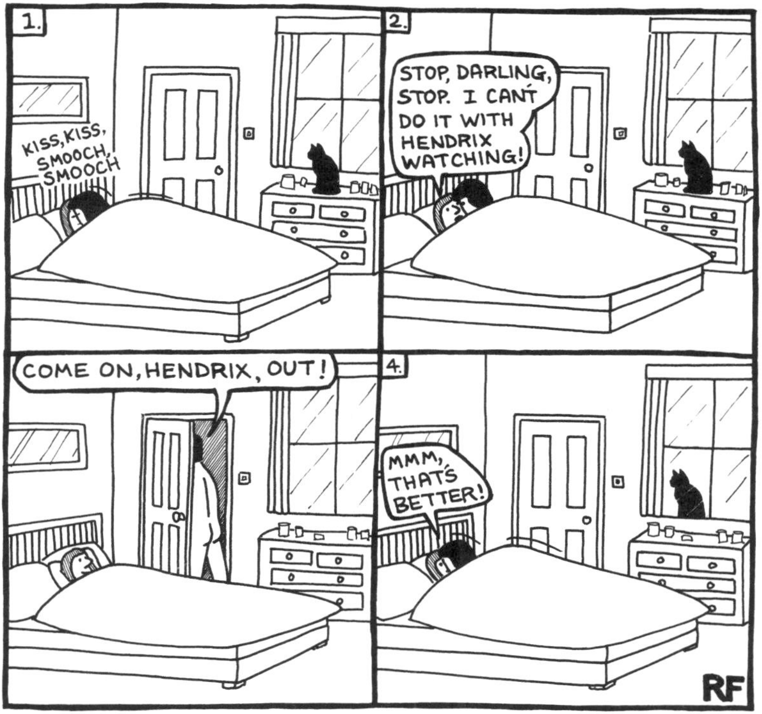
1.
KISS, KISS, SMOOCH, SMOOCH
2.
STOP, DARLING, STOP. I CAN'T DO IT WITH HENDRIX WATCHING!
COME ON, HENDRIX, OUT!
4.
MMM, THAT'S BETTER!
RF

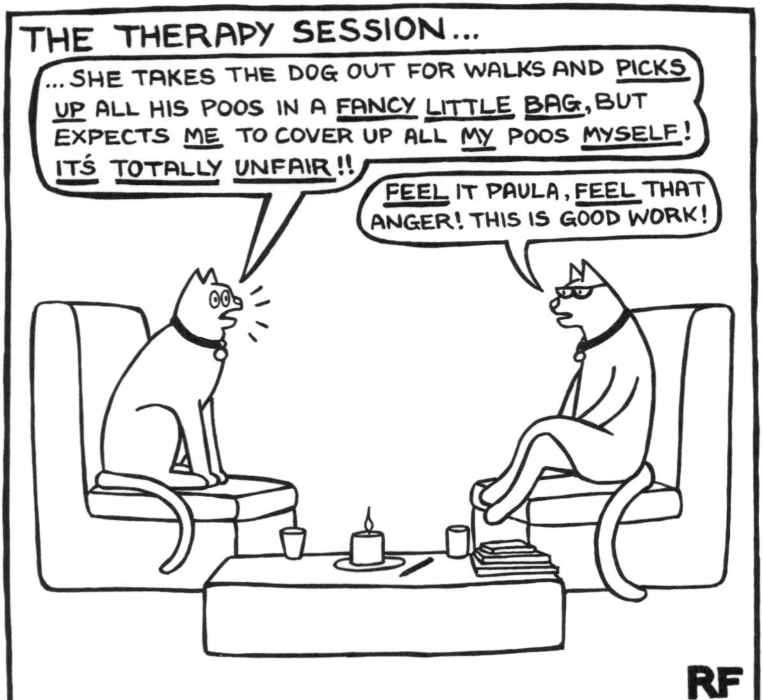
THE THERAPY SESSION...
...SHE TAKES THE DOG OUT FOR WALKS AND PICKS UP ALL HIS POOS IN A FANCY LITTLE BAG, BUT EXPECTS ME TO COVER UP ALL MY POOS MYSELF! IT'S TOTALLY UNFAIR!!
FEEL IT PAULA, FEEL THAT ANGER! THIS IS GOOD WORK!
RF

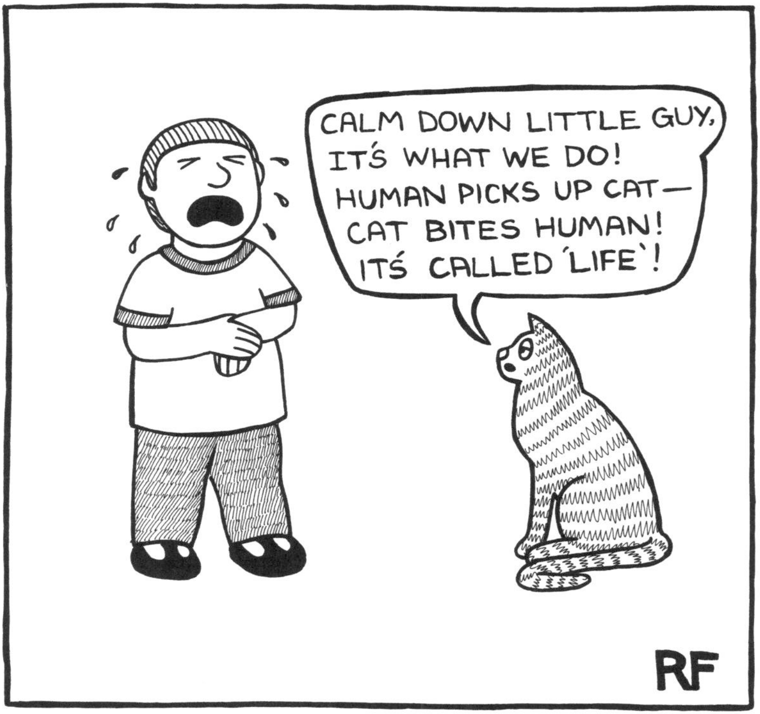
CALM DOWN LITTLE GUY, IT'S WHAT WE DO! HUMAN PICKS UP CAT— CAT BITES HUMAN! IT'S CALLED 'LIFE'!
RF

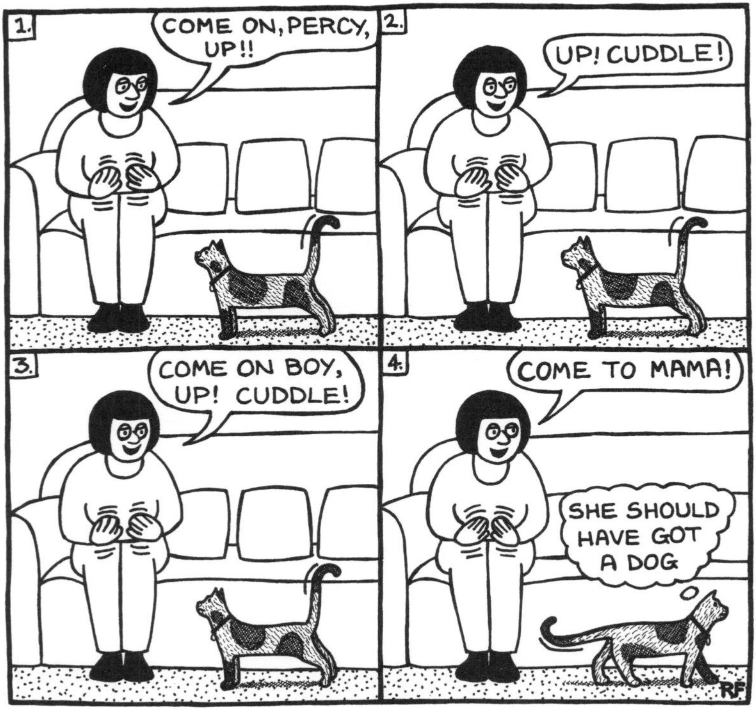
1.
COME ON, PERCY, UP!!
2.
UP! CUDDLE!
3.
COME ON BOY, UP! CUDDLE!
4.
COME TO MAMA!
SHE SHOULD HAVE GOT A DOG
RF

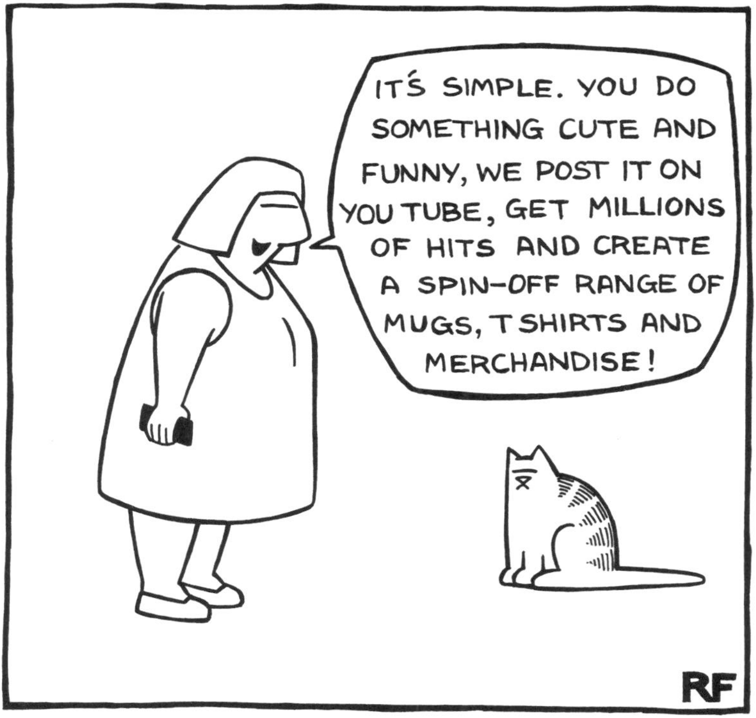
IT'S SIMPLE. YOU DO SOMETHING CUTE AND FUNNY, WE POST IT ON YOU TUBE, GET MILLIONS OF HITS AND CREATE A SPIN-OFF RANGE OF MUGS, T SHIRTS AND MERCHANDISE!
RF

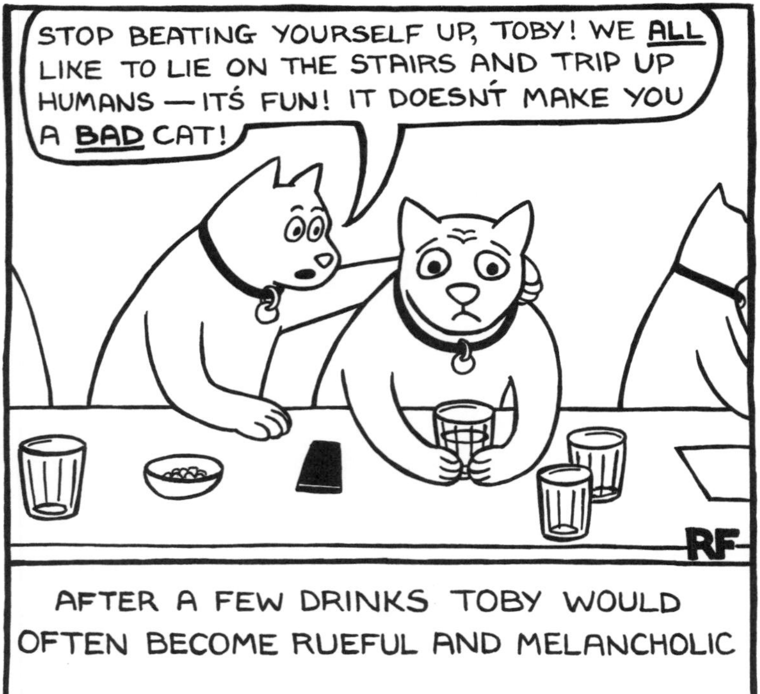
STOP BEATING YOURSELF UP, TOBY! WE ALL LIKE TO LIE ON THE STAIRS AND TRIP UP HUMANS — IT'S FUN! IT DOESN'T MAKE YOU A BAD CAT!
RF
AFTER A FEW DRINKS TOBY WOULD OFTEN BECOME RUEFUL AND MELANCHOLIC

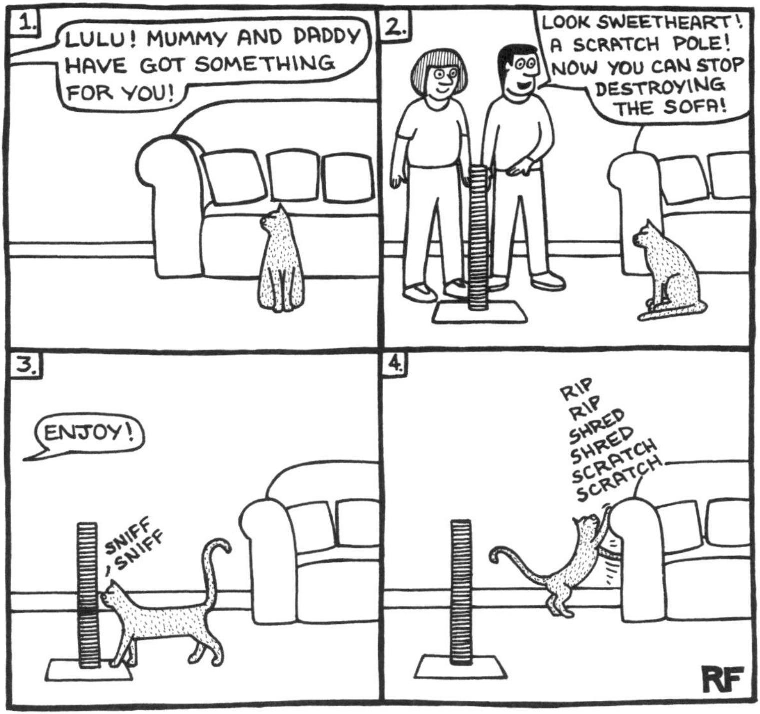
1.
LULU! MUMMY AND DADDY HAVE GOT SOMETHING FOR YOU!
2.
LOOK SWEETHEART! A SCRATCH POLE! NOW YOU CAN STOP DESTROYING THE SOFA!
3.
ENJOY!
SNIFF, SNIFF
4.
RIP
RIP
SHRED
SHRED
SCRATCH
SCRATCH
RF

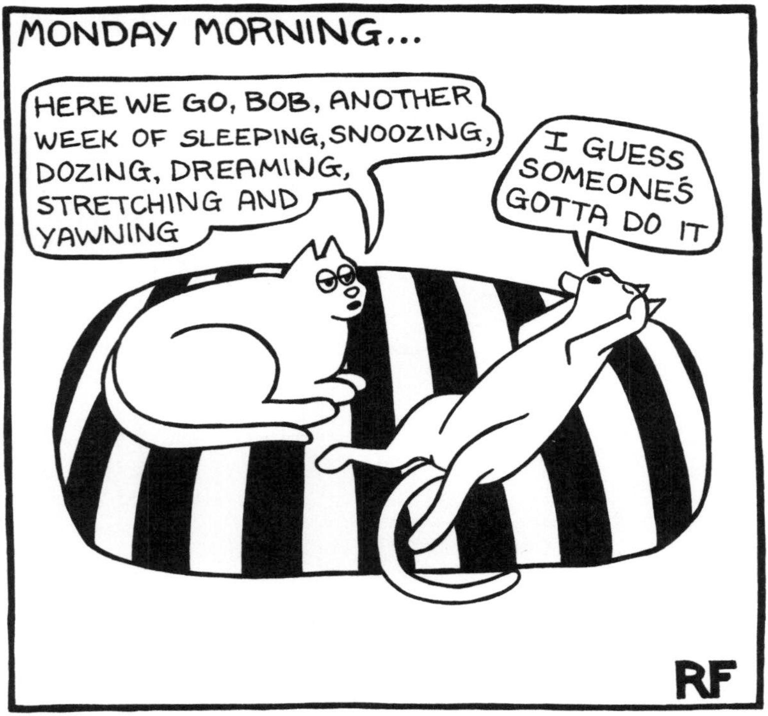
MONDAY MORNING...
HERE WE GO, BOB, ANOTHER WEEK OF SLEEPING, SNOOZING, DOZING, DREAMING, STRETCHING AND YAWNING
I GUESS SOMEONE'S GOTTA DO IT
RF

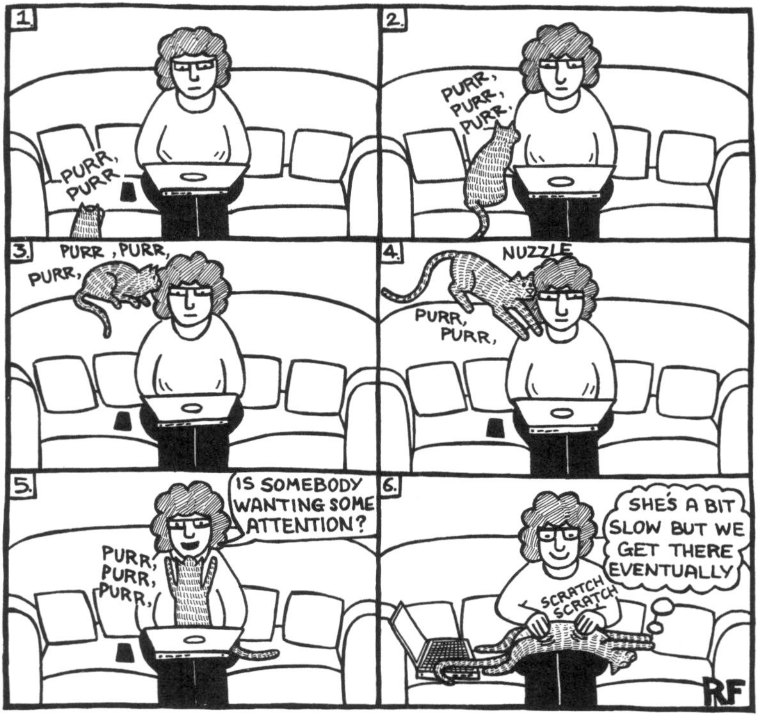
1.
PURR, PURR
2.
PURR, PURR, PURR,
3.
PURR, PURR, PURR,
4.
NUZZLE
PURR, PURR,
5.
IS SOMEBODY WANTING SOME ATTENTION?
PURR, PURR, PURR,
6.
SHE'S A BIT SLOW BUT WE GET THERE EVENTUALLY
SCRATCH SCRATCH
RF

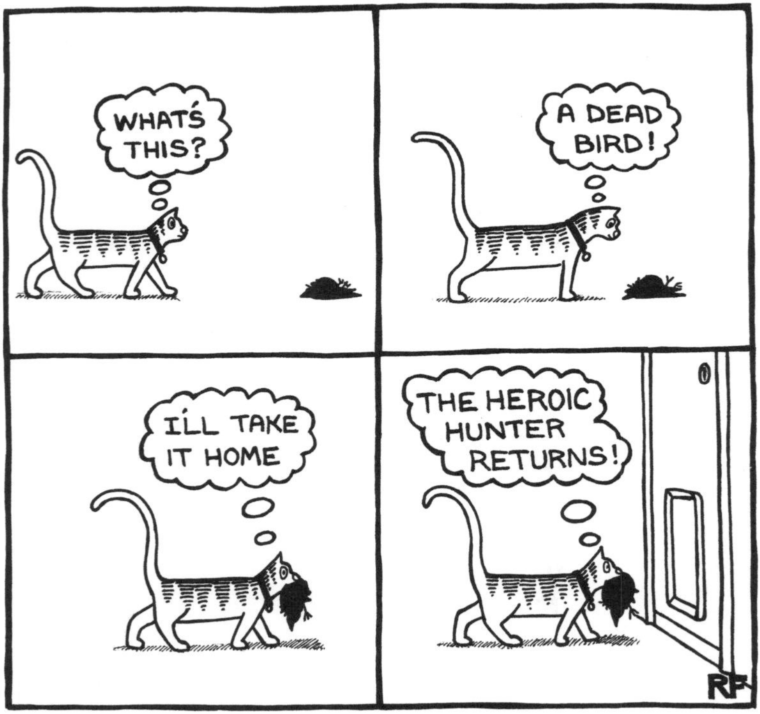
WHATŚ THIS?
A DEAD BIRD!
IĹL TAKE IT HOME
THE HEROIC HUNTER RETURNS!
RF

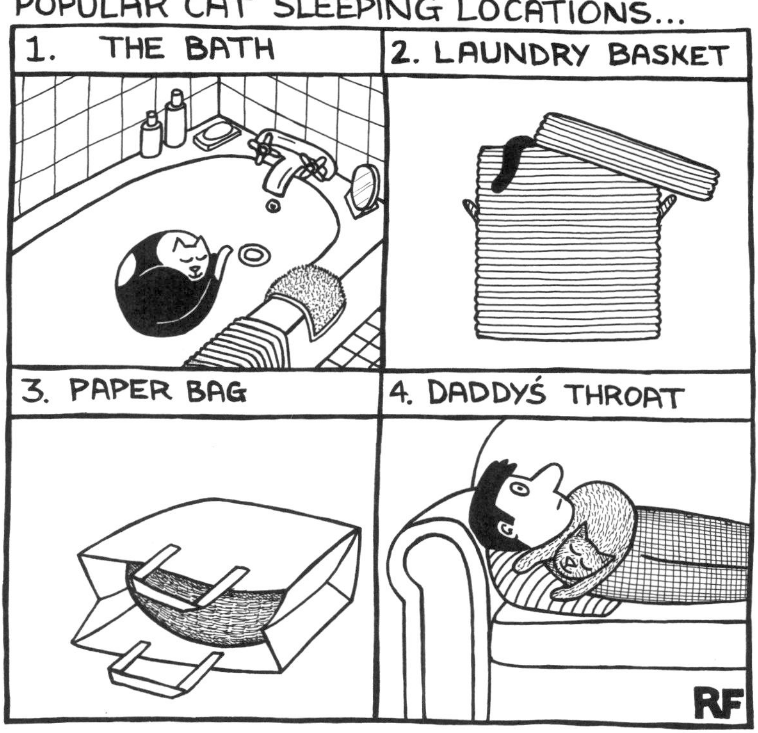
POPULAR CAT SLEEPING LOCATIONS...
1. THE BATH
2. LAUNDRY BASKET
3. PAPER BAG
4. DADDY'S THROAT
RF

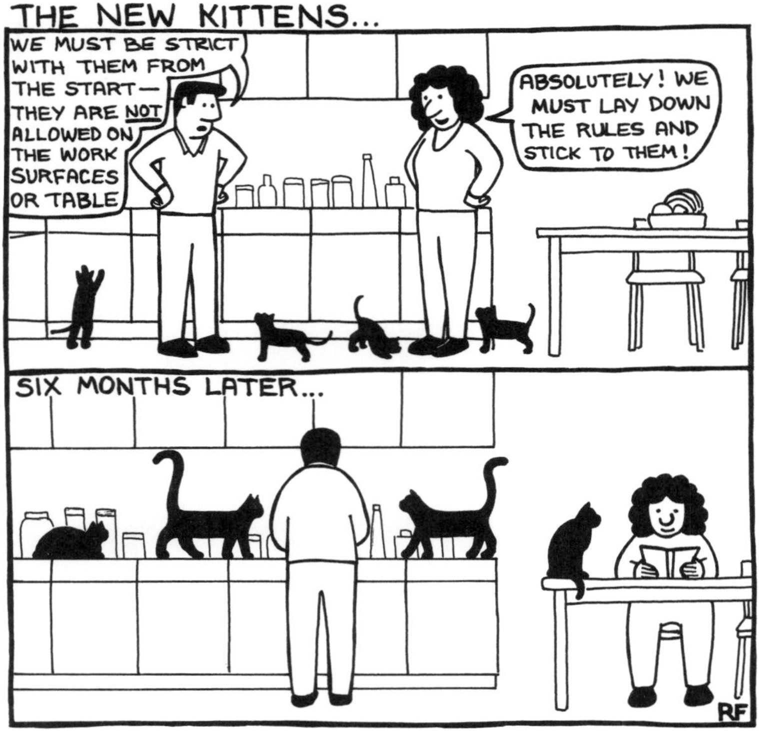
THE NEW KITTENS...
WE MUST BE STRICT WITH THEM FROM THE START— THEY ARE NOT ALLOWED ON THE WORK SURFACES OR TABLE
ABSOLUTELY! WE MUST LAY DOWN THE RULES AND STICK TO THEM!
SIX MONTHS LATER...
RF

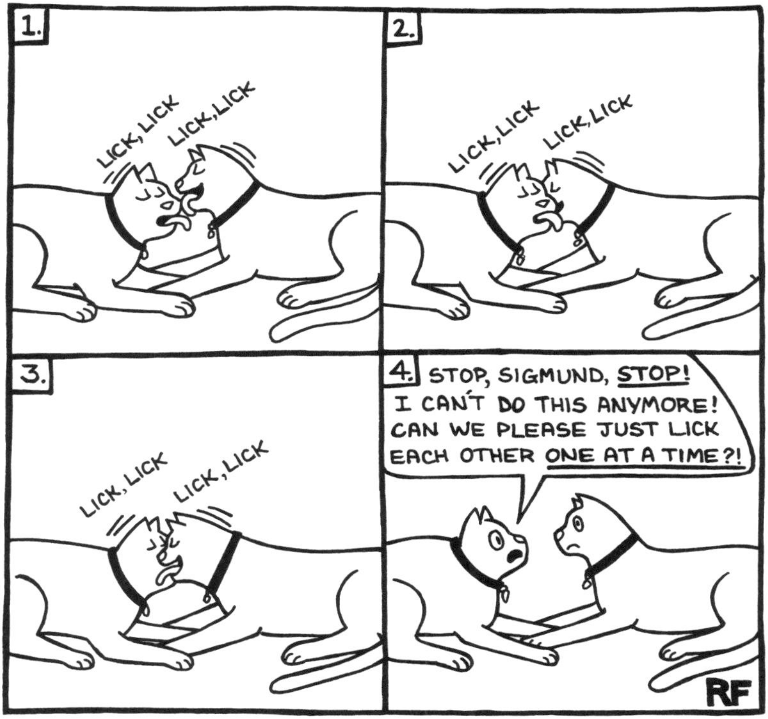
1.
LICK, LICK
LICK, LICK
2.
LICK, LICK
LICK, LICK
3.
LICK, LICK
LICK, LICK
4.
STOP, SIGMUND, STOP! I CAN'T DO THIS ANYMORE! CAN WE PLEASE JUST LICK EACH OTHER ONE AT A TIME?!
RF

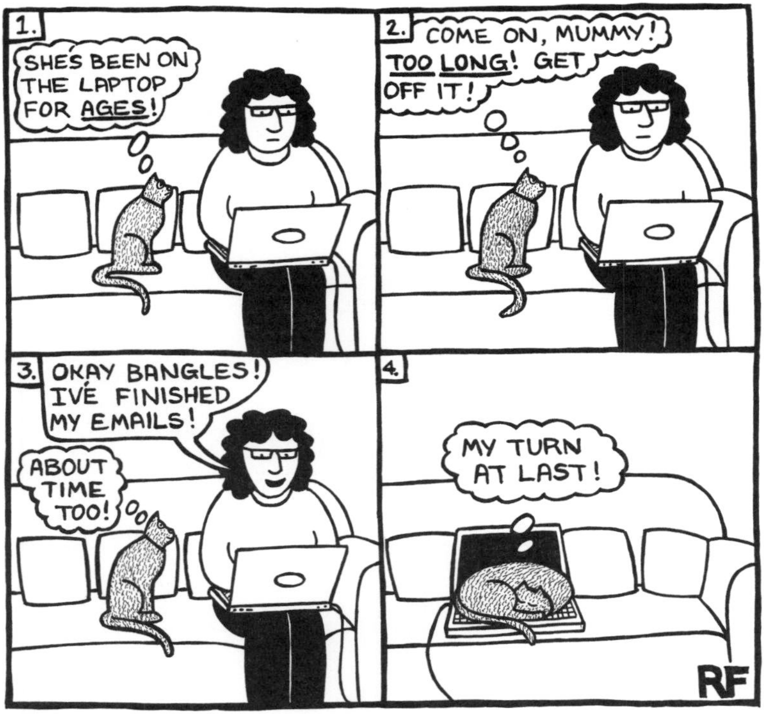
1.
SHE'S BEEN ON THE LAPTOP FOR AGES!
2.
COME ON, MUMMY! TOO LONG! GET OFF IT!
3.
OKAY BANGLES! I'VE FINISHED MY EMAILS!
ABOUT TIME TOO!
4.
MY TURN AT LAST!
RF

THE LITTLE HUNTER...

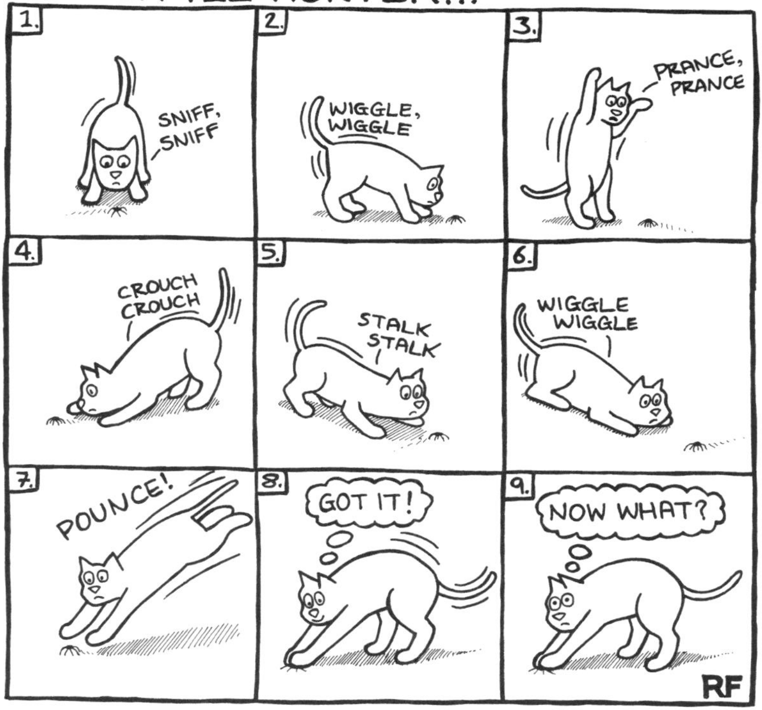
1.
SNIFF, SNIFF
2.
WIGGLE, WIGGLE
3.
PRANCE, PRANCE
4.
CROUCH CROUCH
5.
STALK STALK
6.
WIGGLE WIGGLE
7.
POUNCE!
8.
GOT IT!
9.
NOW WHAT?
RF

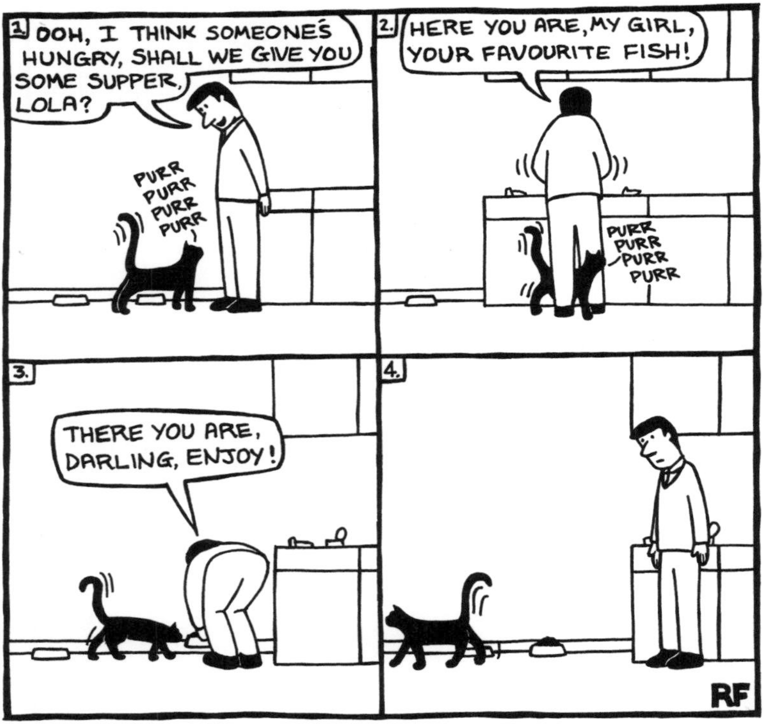
1.
OOH, I THINK SOMEONE'S HUNGRY, SHALL WE GIVE YOU SOME SUPPER, LOLA?
PURR PURR PURR PURR
2.
HERE YOU ARE, MY GIRL, YOUR FAVOURITE FISH!
PURR PURR PURR PURR
3.
THERE YOU ARE, DARLING, ENJOY!
4.
RF

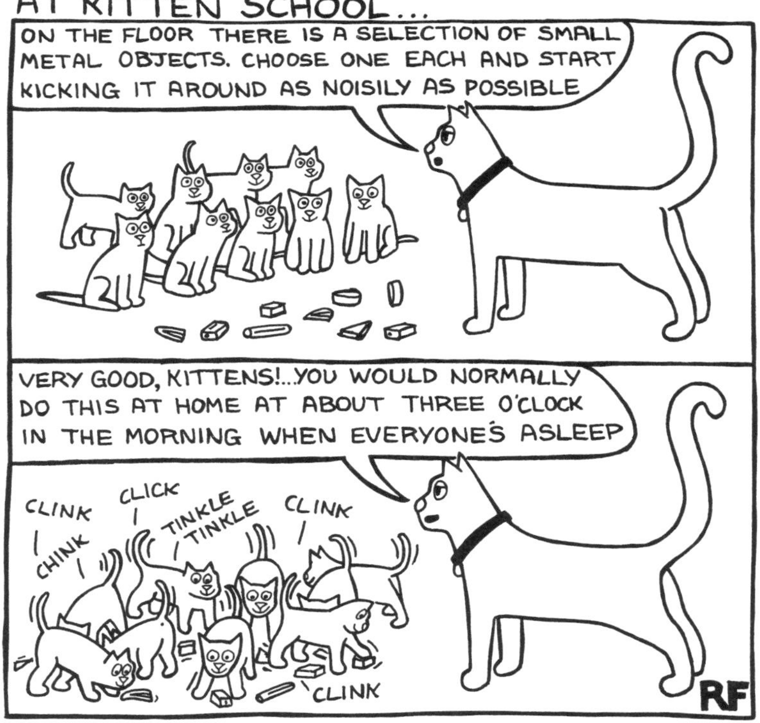
AT KITTEN SCHOOL...
ON THE FLOOR THERE IS A SELECTION OF SMALL METAL OBJECTS. CHOOSE ONE EACH AND START KICKING IT AROUND AS NOISILY AS POSSIBLE
VERY GOOD, KITTENS!...YOU WOULD NORMALLY DO THIS AT HOME AT ABOUT THREE O'CLOCK IN THE MORNING WHEN EVERYONE'S ASLEEP
CLINK
CLICK
TINKLE
TINKLE
CLINK
CHINK
CLINK
RF

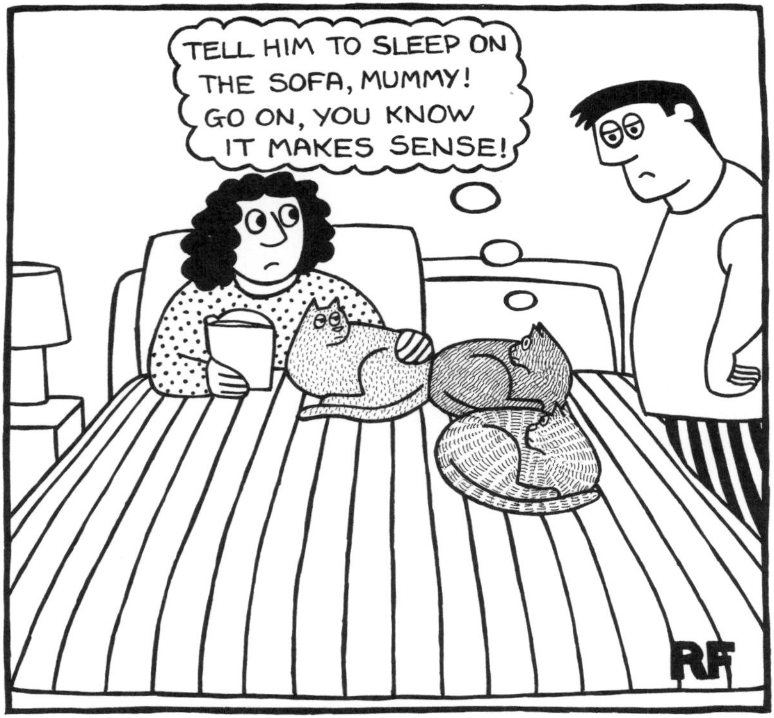
TELL HIM TO SLEEP ON THE SOFA, MUMMY! GO ON, YOU KNOW IT MAKES SENSE!
RF

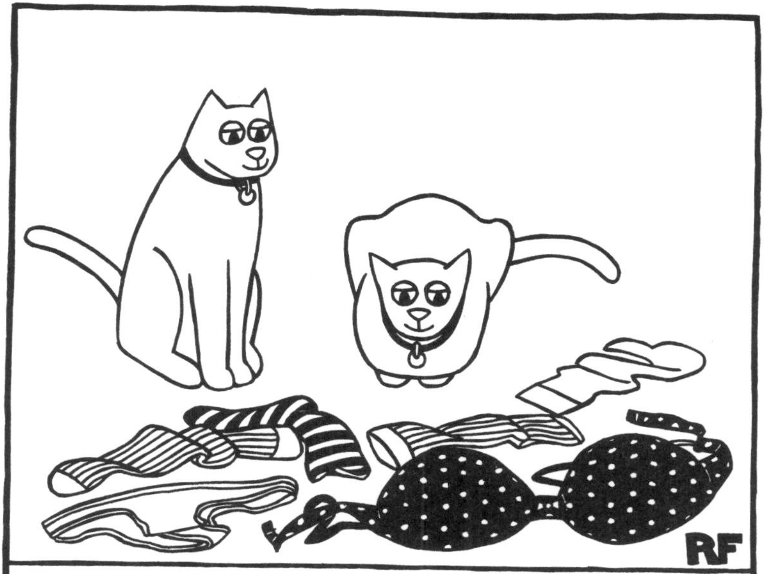
RF

IT HAD BEEN A SUCCESSFUL MORNING'S HUNTING — FOUR SOCKS, ONE PAIR OF KNICKERS AND A SPOTTY DOUBLE D

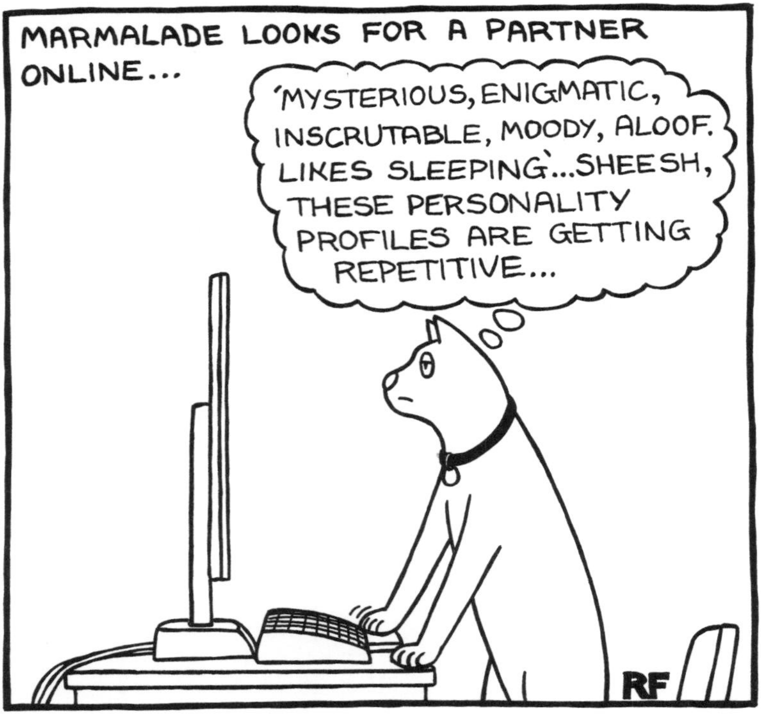
MARMALADE LOOKS FOR A PARTNER ONLINE...
'MYSTERIOUS, ENIGMATIC, INSCRUTABLE, MOODY, ALOOF. LIKES SLEEPING'...SHEESH, THESE PERSONALITY PROFILES ARE GETTING REPETITIVE...
RF

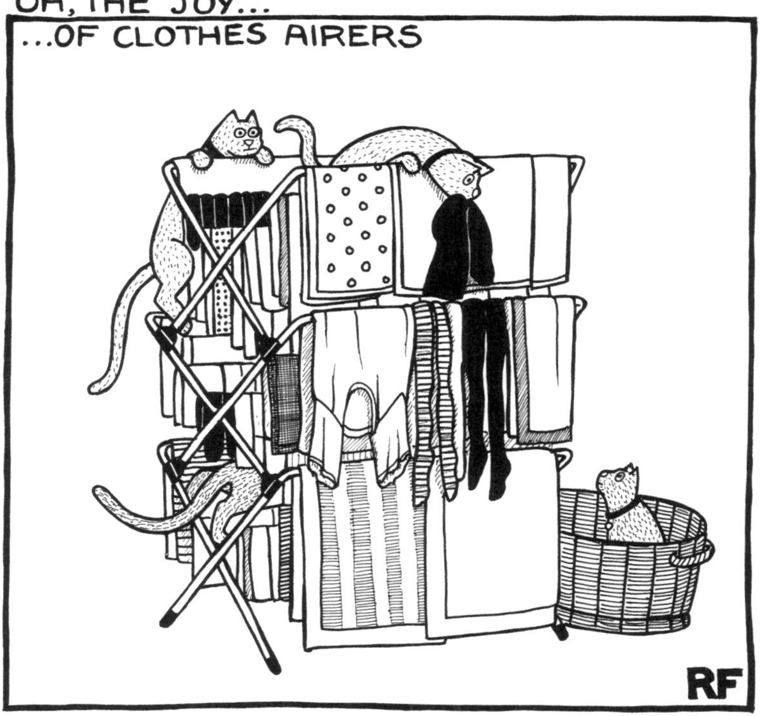
OH, THE JOY...
...OF CLOTHES AIRERS
RF

RECOGNISING CAT FACIAL EXPRESSIONS...
1.
'I NEED SOME LOVE.'
2.
'I'M HUNGRY.'
3.
'I'M GOING TO RUN ALL OVER THE HOUSE AND GO COMPLETELY CRAZY.'
4.
'HUMANS ARE IDIOTS.'
RF

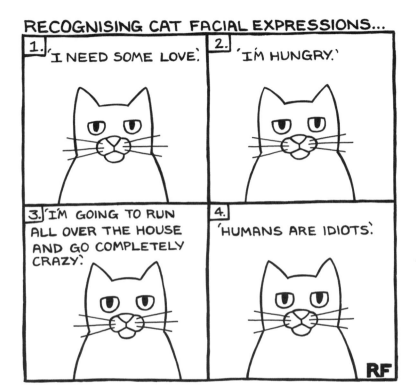

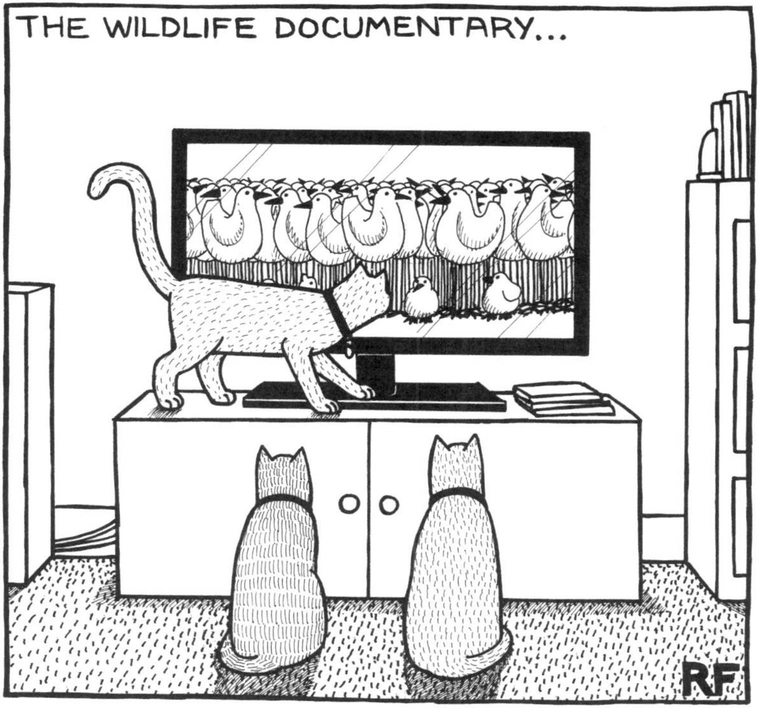
THE WILDLIFE DOCUMENTARY...
RF

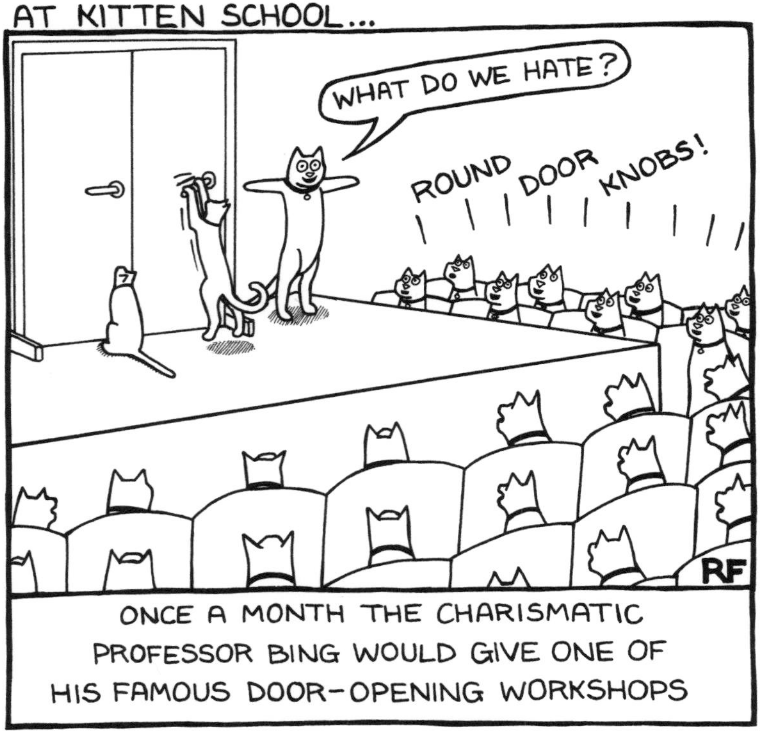
AT KITTEN SCHOOL...
WHAT DO WE HATE?
ROUND DOOR KNOBS!
RF
ONCE A MONTH THE CHARISMATIC PROFESSOR BING WOULD GIVE ONE OF HIS FAMOUS DOOR-OPENING WORKSHOPS

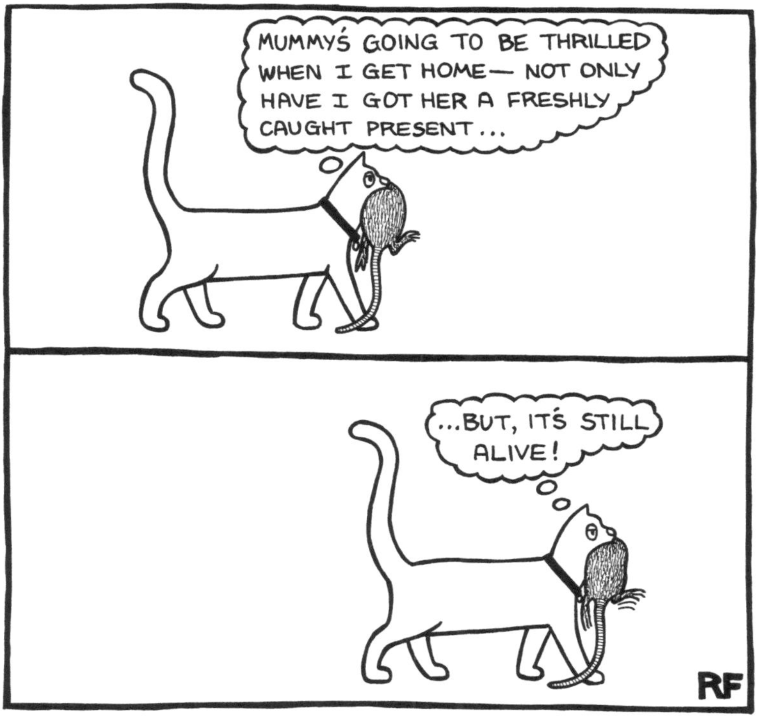
MUMMY'S GOING TO BE THRILLED WHEN I GET HOME— NOT ONLY HAVE I GOT HER A FRESHLY CAUGHT PRESENT...
...BUT, IT'S STILL ALIVE!
RF

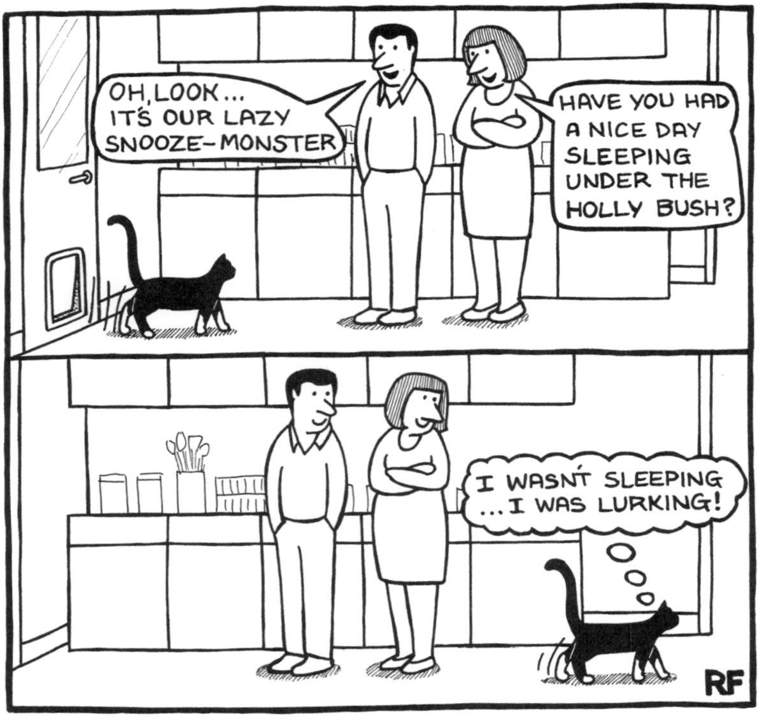
OH, LOOK...
IT'S OUR LAZY
SNOOZE-MONSTER
HAVE YOU HAD
A NICE DAY
SLEEPING
UNDER THE
HOLLY BUSH?
I WASN'T SLEEPING
...I WAS LURKING!
RF

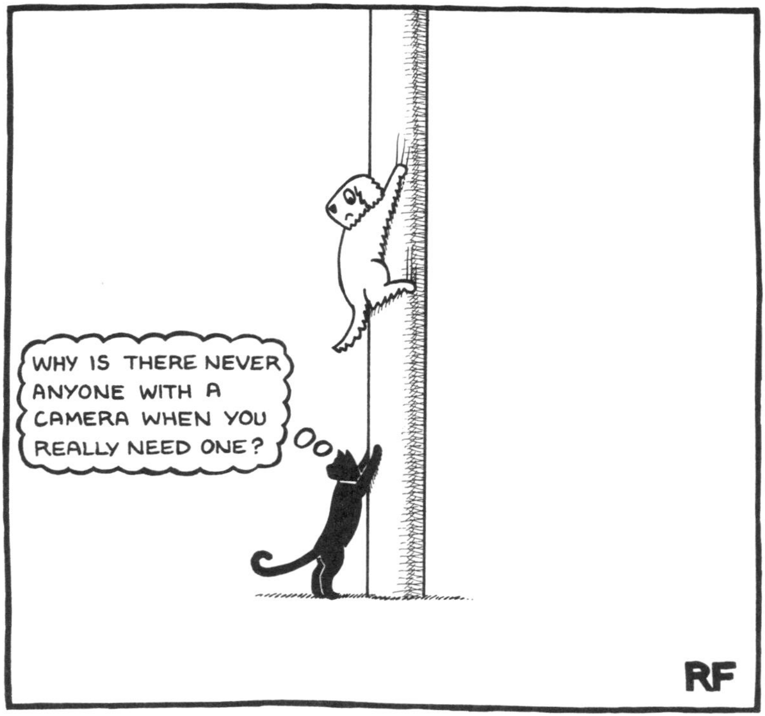
WHY IS THERE NEVER ANYONE WITH A CAMERA WHEN YOU REALLY NEED ONE?
RF

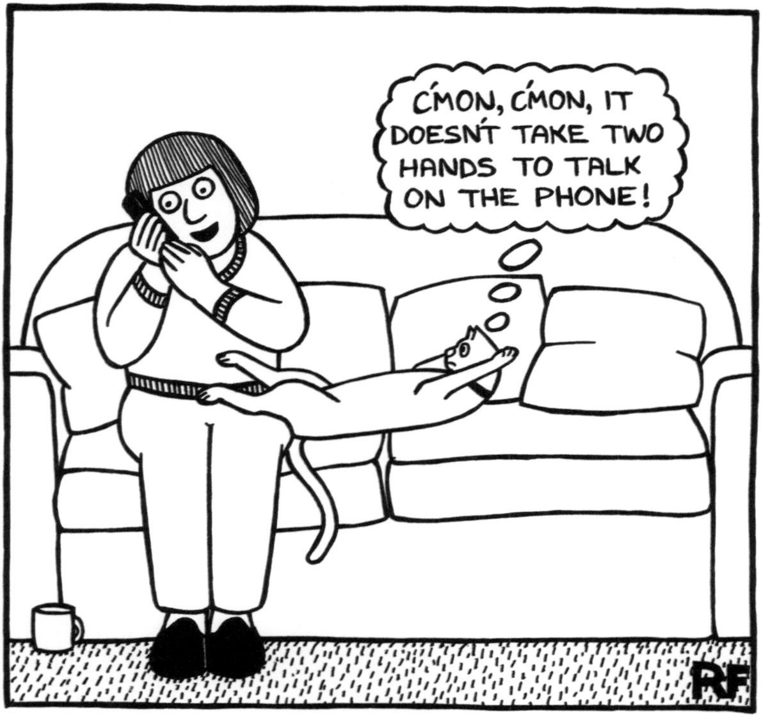
C'MON, C'MON, IT DOESN'T TAKE TWO HANDS TO TALK ON THE PHONE!
RF

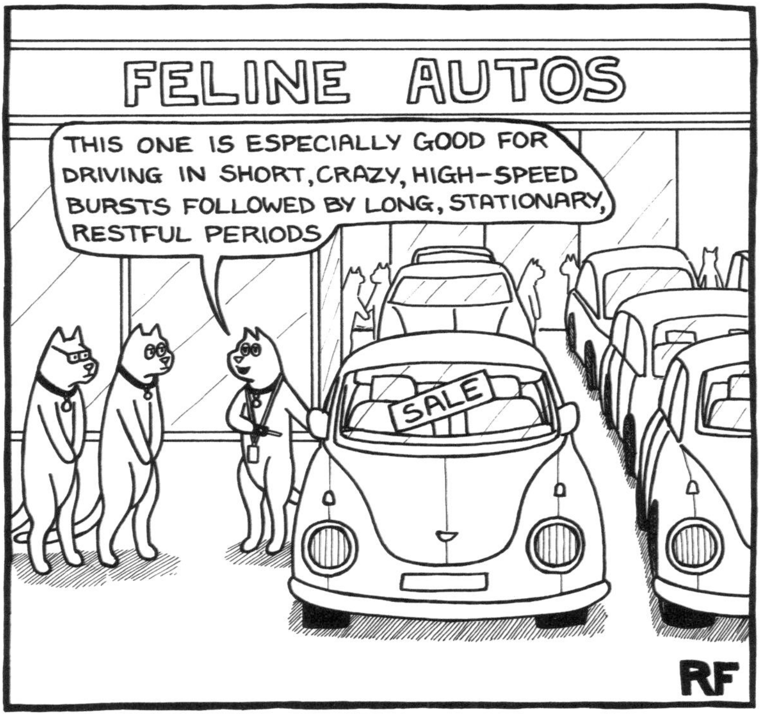
FELINE AUTOS
THIS ONE IS ESPECIALLY GOOD FOR DRIVING IN SHORT, CRAZY, HIGH-SPEED BURSTS FOLLOWED BY LONG, STATIONARY, RESTFUL PERIODS
SALE
RF

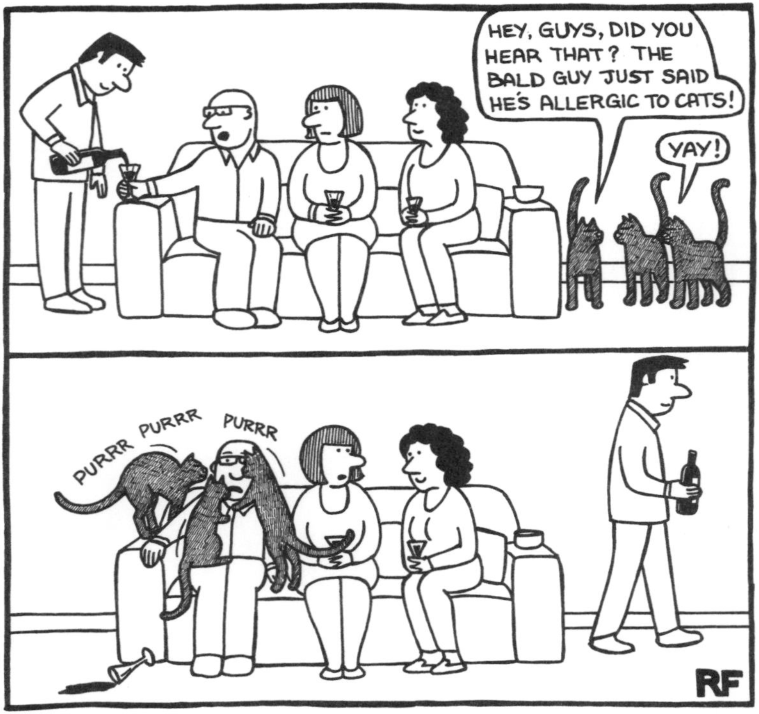
HEY, GUYS, DID YOU HEAR THAT? THE BALD GUY JUST SAID HE'S ALLERGIC TO CATS!
YAY!
PURRR
PURRR
PURRR
RF

FOUR REASONS TO NEVER TRUST A HUMAN

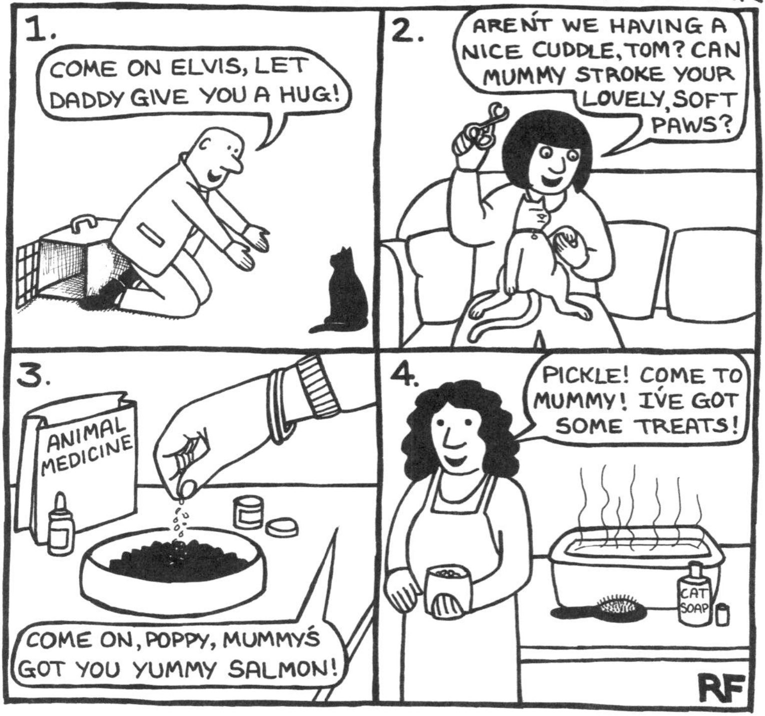
1.
COME ON ELVIS, LET DADDY GIVE YOU A HUG!
2.
AREN'T WE HAVING A NICE CUDDLE, TOM? CAN MUMMY STROKE YOUR LOVELY, SOFT PAWS?
3.
ANIMAL MEDICINE
COME ON, POPPY, MUMMY'S GOT YOU YUMMY SALMON!
4.
PICKLE! COME TO MUMMY! I'VE GOT SOME TREATS!
CAT SOAP
RF

WHEN THE CAT IS READY...
8 a.m.
CUDDLE?
NOPE
10 a.m.
CUDDLE?
NOPE
12 p.m.
CUDDLE?
NOPE
2 p.m.
CUDDLE?
NOPE
4 p.m.
CUDDLE?
NOPE
6 p.m.
PURR PURR
CUDDLE?
RF

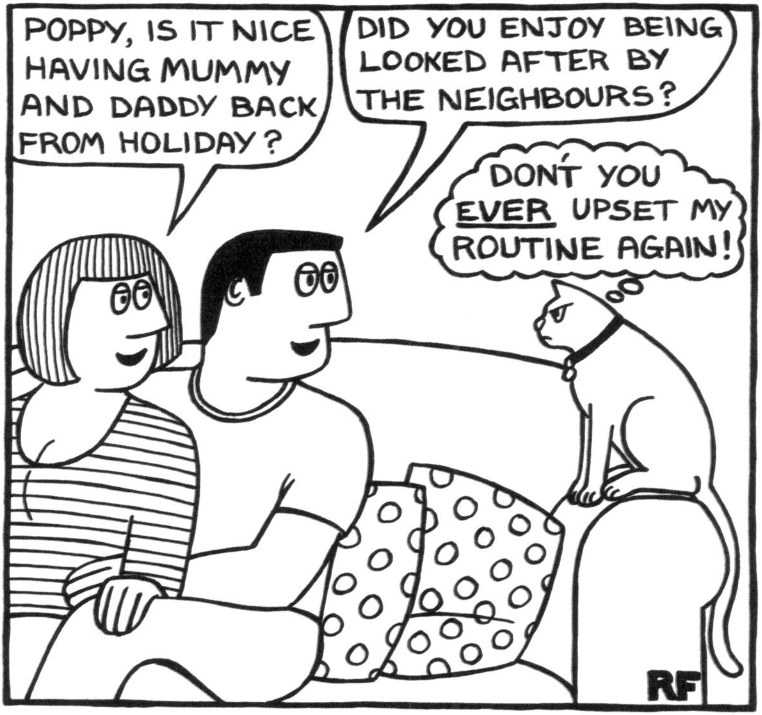
POPPY, IS IT NICE HAVING MUMMY AND DADDY BACK FROM HOLIDAY?
DID YOU ENJOY BEING LOOKED AFTER BY THE NEIGHBOURS?
DON'T YOU EVER UPSET MY ROUTINE AGAIN!
RF

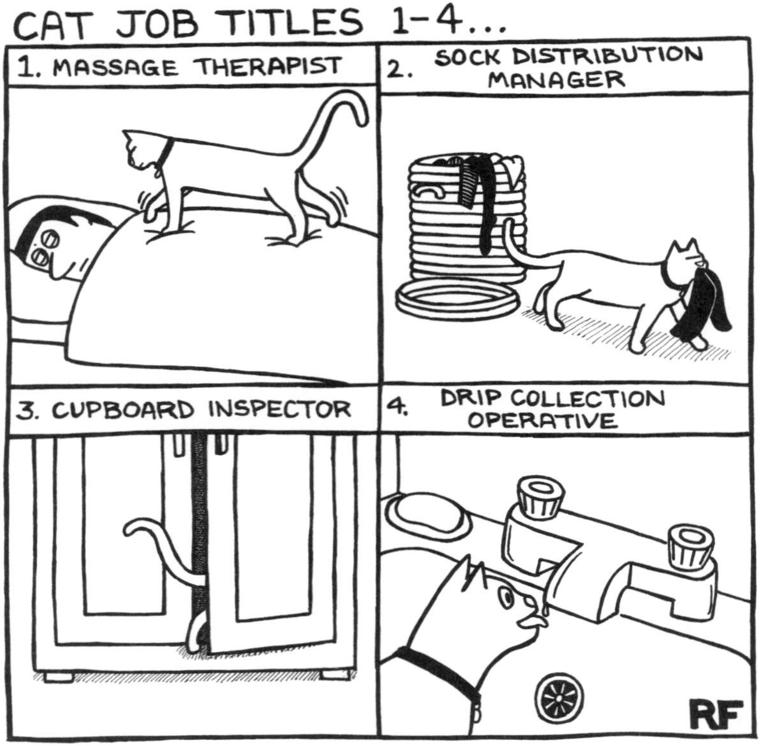
CAT JOB TITLES 1-4...
1. MASSAGE THERAPIST
2. SOCK DISTRIBUTION MANAGER
3. CUPBOARD INSPECTOR
4. DRIP COLLECTION OPERATIVE
RF

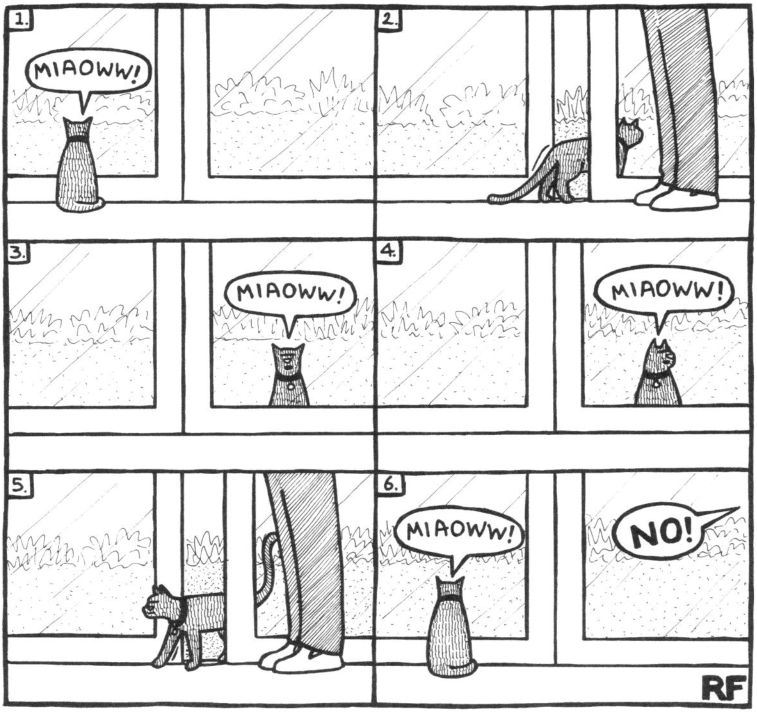
1.
MIAOWW!
2.
3.
MIAOWW!
4.
MIAOWW!
5.
6.
MIAOWW!
NO!
RF

AT KITTEN SCHOOL...

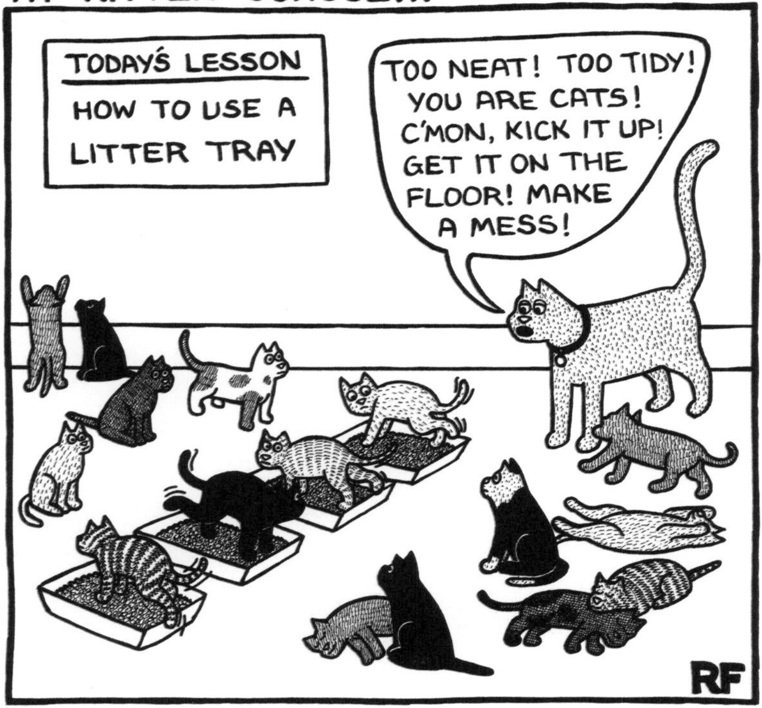

HIERARCHY OF AN ANIMAL-LOVING FAMILY...

1. THE CAT
2. MUM
3. THE DOG
4. THE KIDS
5. THE RABBIT
6. DAD

RF

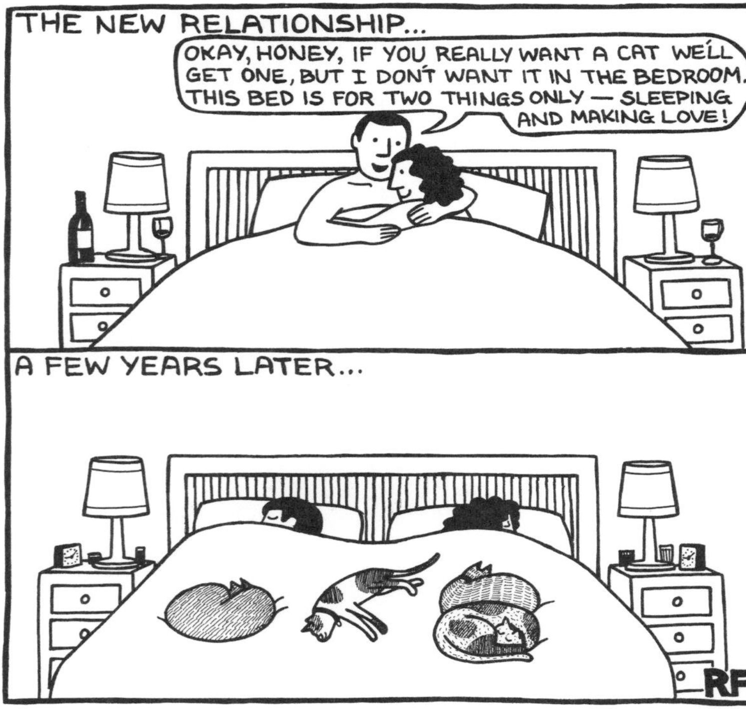
THE NEW RELATIONSHIP...
OKAY, HONEY, IF YOU REALLY WANT A CAT WE'LL GET ONE, BUT I DON'T WANT IT IN THE BEDROOM. THIS BED IS FOR TWO THINGS ONLY — SLEEPING AND MAKING LOVE!
A FEW YEARS LATER...
RF

AT KITTEN SCHOOL...

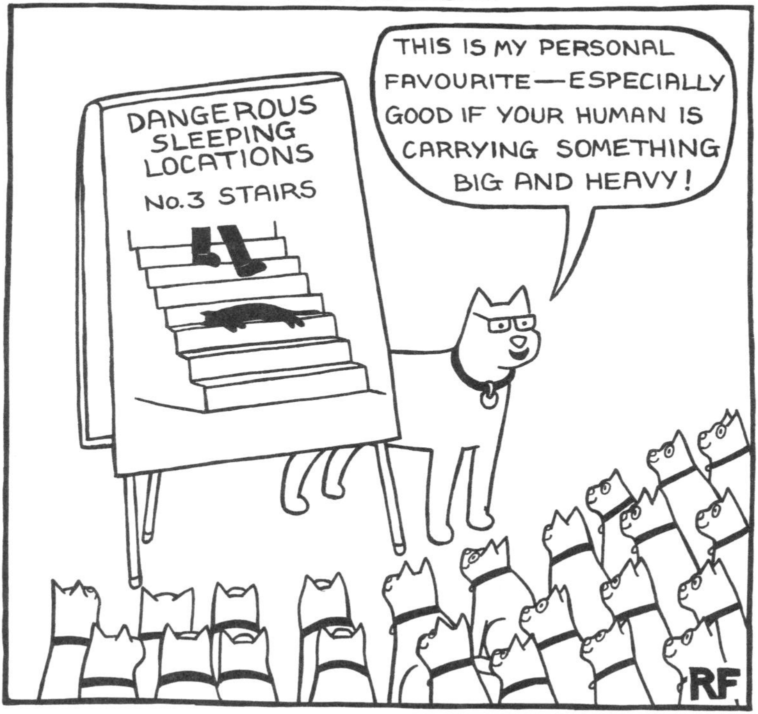
DANGEROUS SLEEPING LOCATIONS
No.3 STAIRS
THIS IS MY PERSONAL FAVOURITE—ESPECIALLY GOOD IF YOUR HUMAN IS CARRYING SOMETHING BIG AND HEAVY!
RF

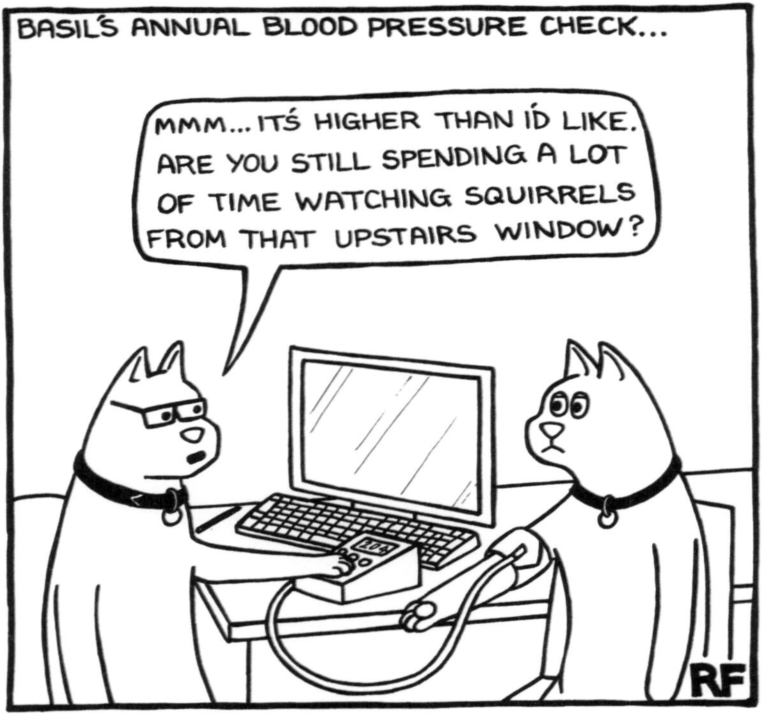
BASIL'S ANNUAL BLOOD PRESSURE CHECK...
MMM... IT'S HIGHER THAN I'D LIKE. ARE YOU STILL SPENDING A LOT OF TIME WATCHING SQUIRRELS FROM THAT UPSTAIRS WINDOW?
204
RF

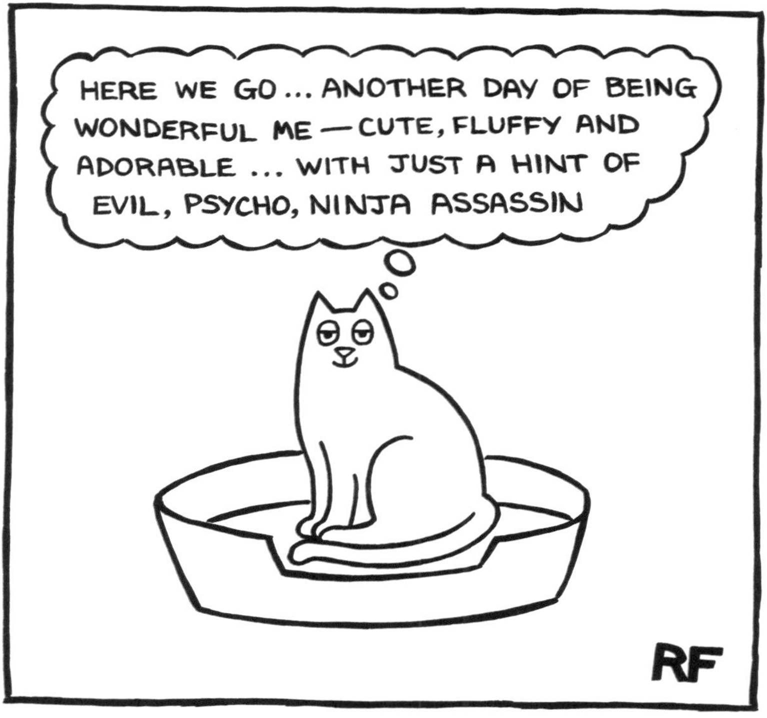
HERE WE GO... ANOTHER DAY OF BEING WONDERFUL ME — CUTE, FLUFFY AND ADORABLE ... WITH JUST A HINT OF EVIL, PSYCHO, NINJA ASSASSIN
RF

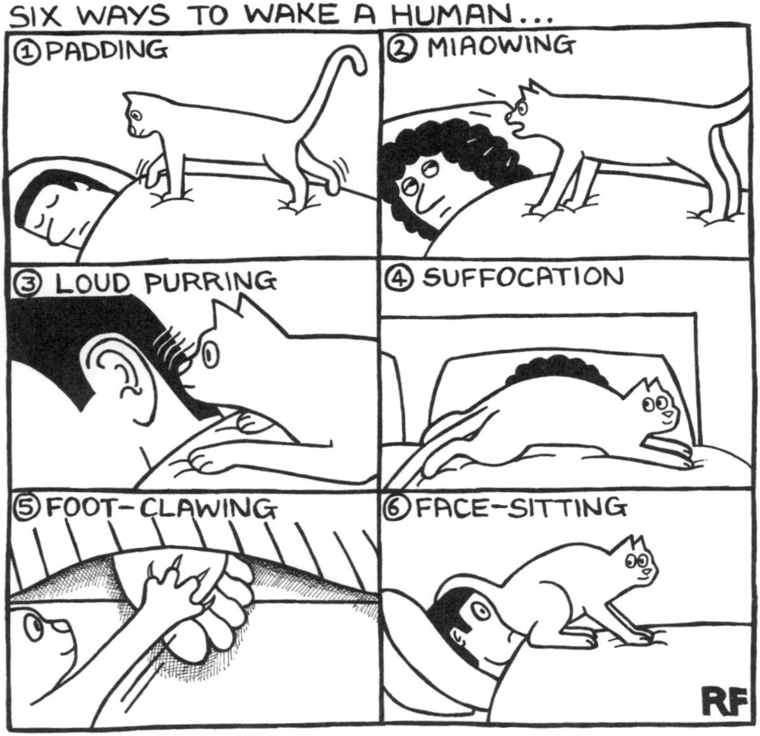
SIX WAYS TO WAKE A HUMAN...
① PADDING
② MIAOWING
③ LOUD PURRING
④ SUFFOCATION
⑤ FOOT-CLAWING
⑥ FACE-SITTING
RF

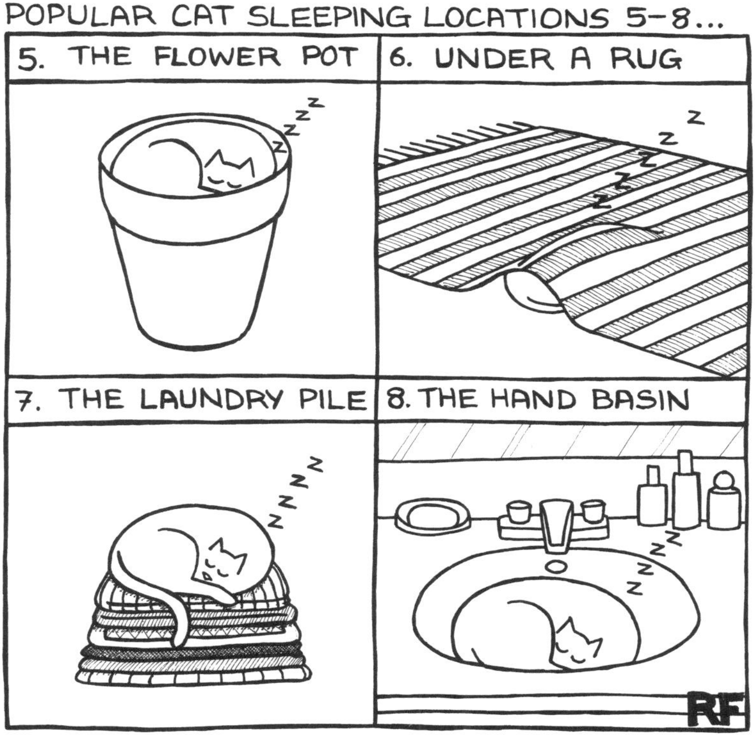
POPULAR CAT SLEEPING LOCATIONS 5–8...
5. THE FLOWER POT
6. UNDER A RUG
7. THE LAUNDRY PILE
8. THE HAND BASIN
RF

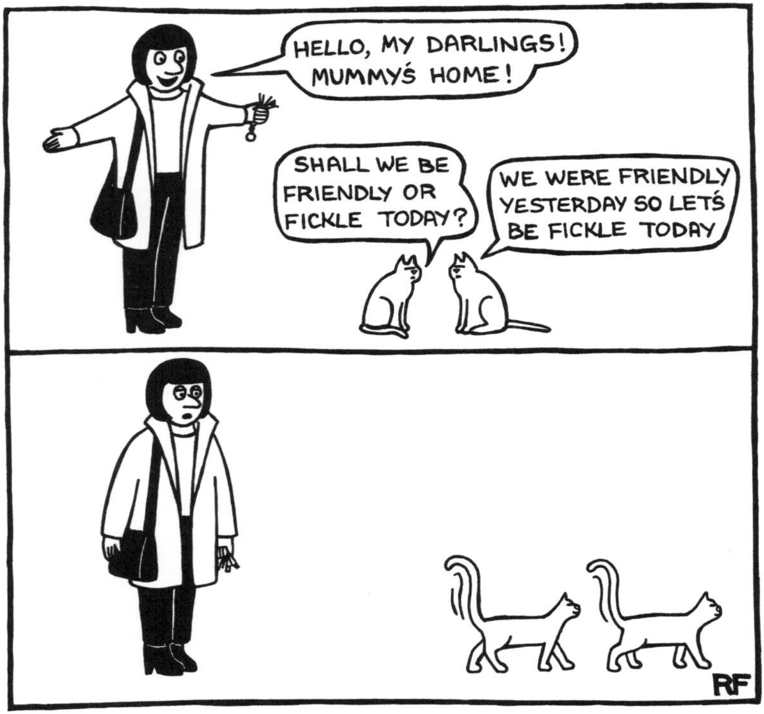
HELLO, MY DARLINGS! MUMMY'S HOME!
SHALL WE BE FRIENDLY OR FICKLE TODAY?
WE WERE FRIENDLY YESTERDAY SO LET'S BE FICKLE TODAY
RF

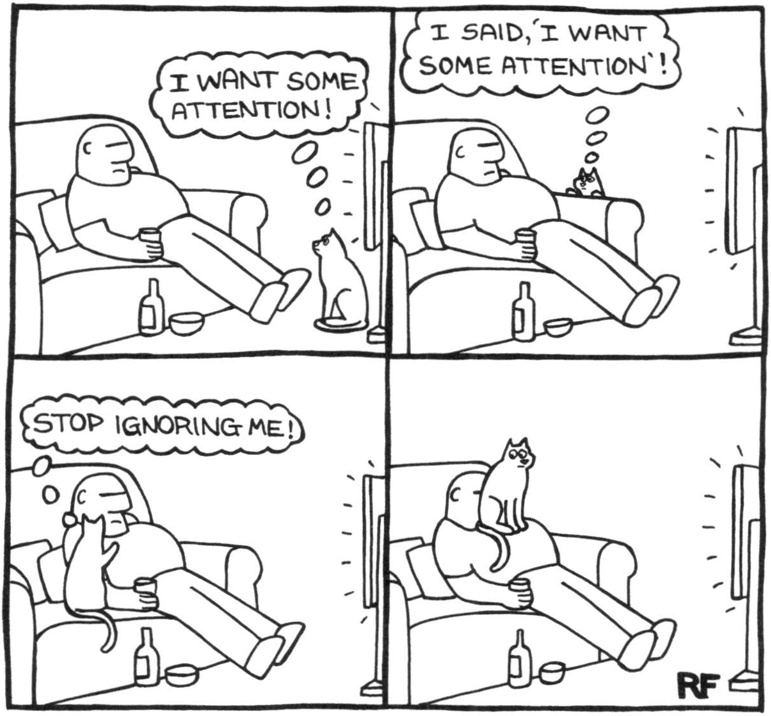
I WANT SOME ATTENTION!
I SAID, 'I WANT SOME ATTENTION'!
STOP IGNORING ME!
RF

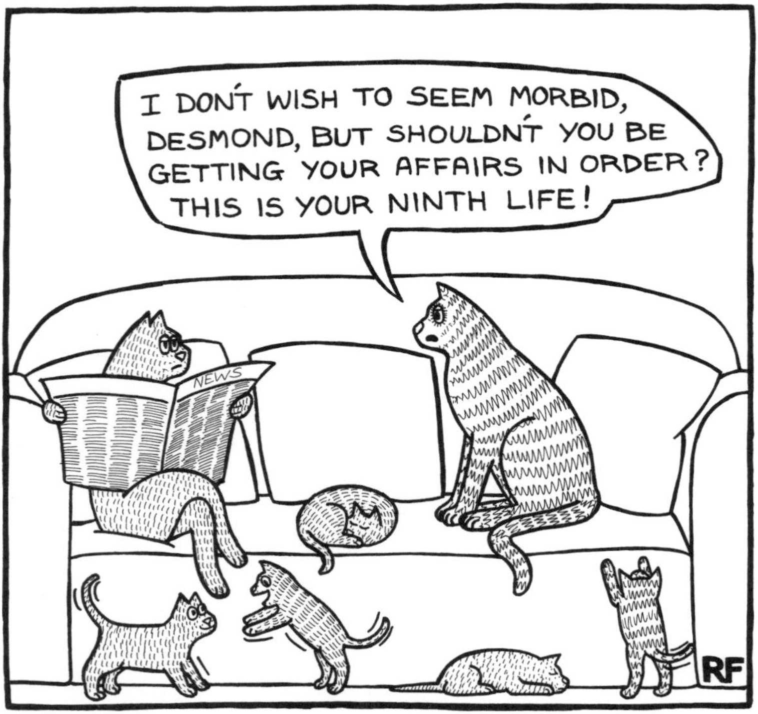
I DON'T WISH TO SEEM MORBID, DESMOND, BUT SHOULDN'T YOU BE GETTING YOUR AFFAIRS IN ORDER? THIS IS YOUR NINTH LIFE!
NEWS
RF

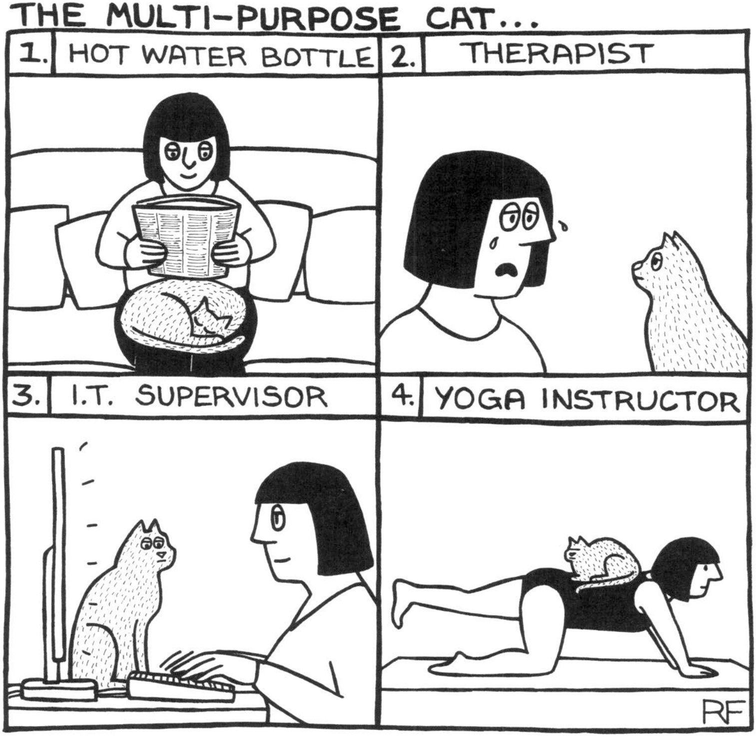
THE MULTI-PURPOSE CAT...
1. HOT WATER BOTTLE
2. THERAPIST
3. I.T. SUPERVISOR
4. YOGA INSTRUCTOR
RF

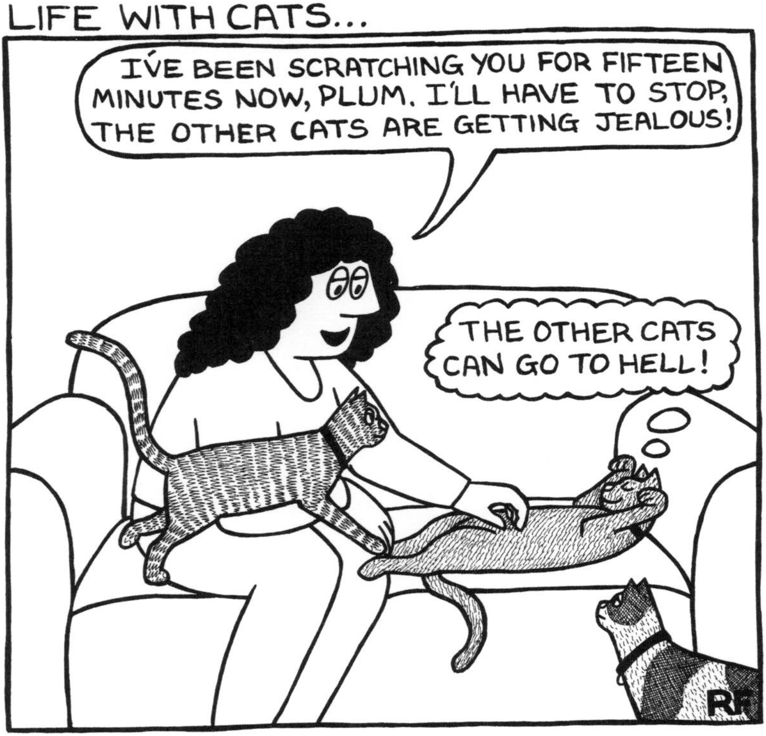
LIFE WITH CATS...
I'VE BEEN SCRATCHING YOU FOR FIFTEEN MINUTES NOW, PLUM. I'LL HAVE TO STOP, THE OTHER CATS ARE GETTING JEALOUS!
THE OTHER CATS CAN GO TO HELL!
RF

PSST, TINA, WAKE UP! IT'S TIME TO JUMP ON THE HUMANS!
WHY? IT'S THE MIDDLE OF THE NIGHT!
THEY ONLY CAME BACK FROM HOLIDAY TWO DAYS AGO AND WE'VE GOT TO PUNISH THEM FOR AT LEAST A WEEK!
RF

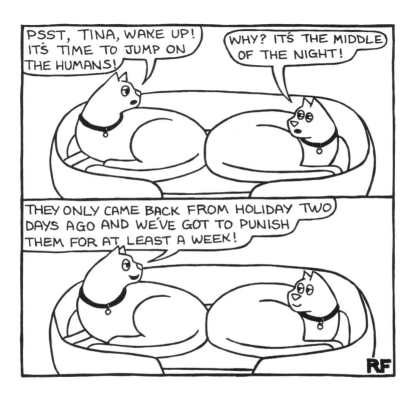

THE ART OF NIGHT-TIME POUNCING 2

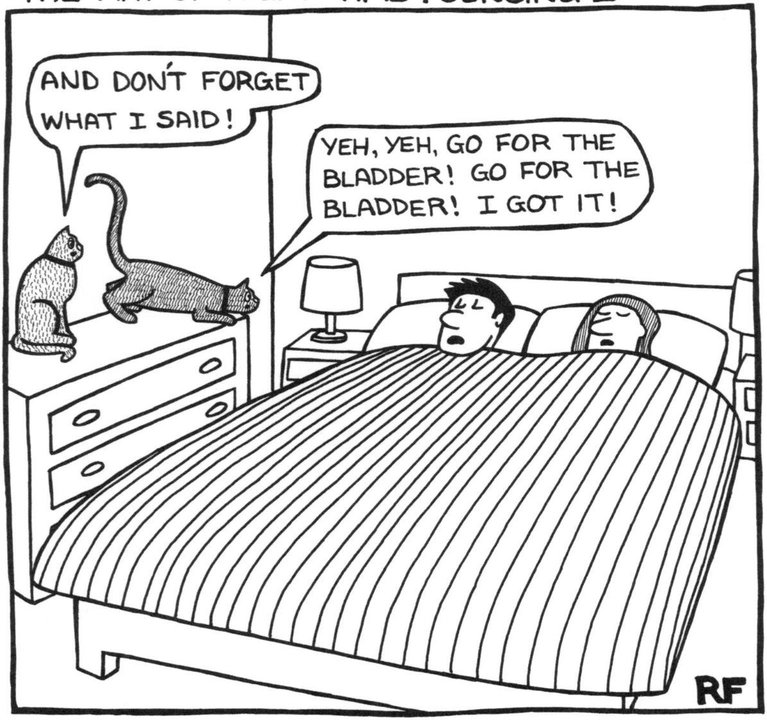
AND DON'T FORGET WHAT I SAID!
YEH, YEH, GO FOR THE BLADDER! GO FOR THE BLADDER! I GOT IT!
RF

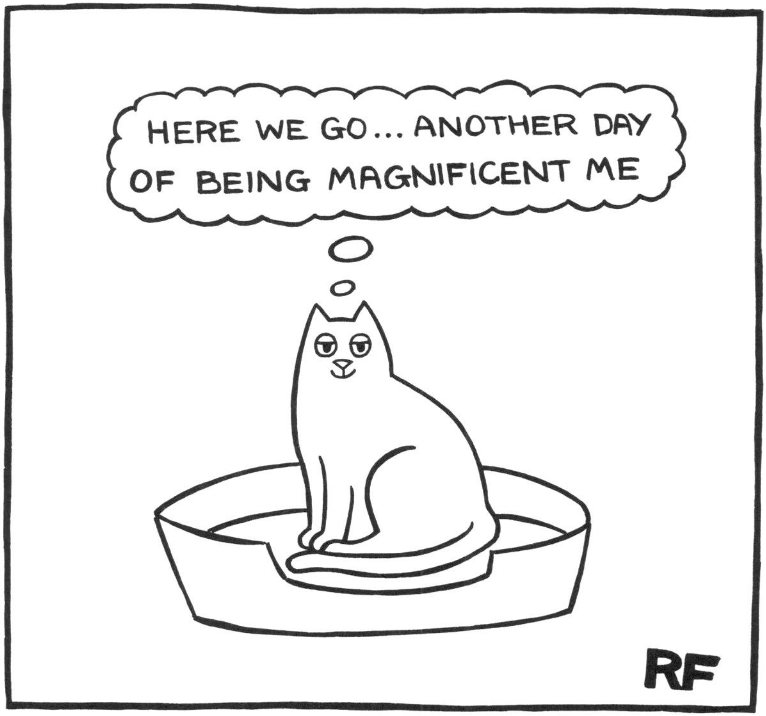
HERE WE GO... ANOTHER DAY OF BEING MAGNIFICENT ME
RF

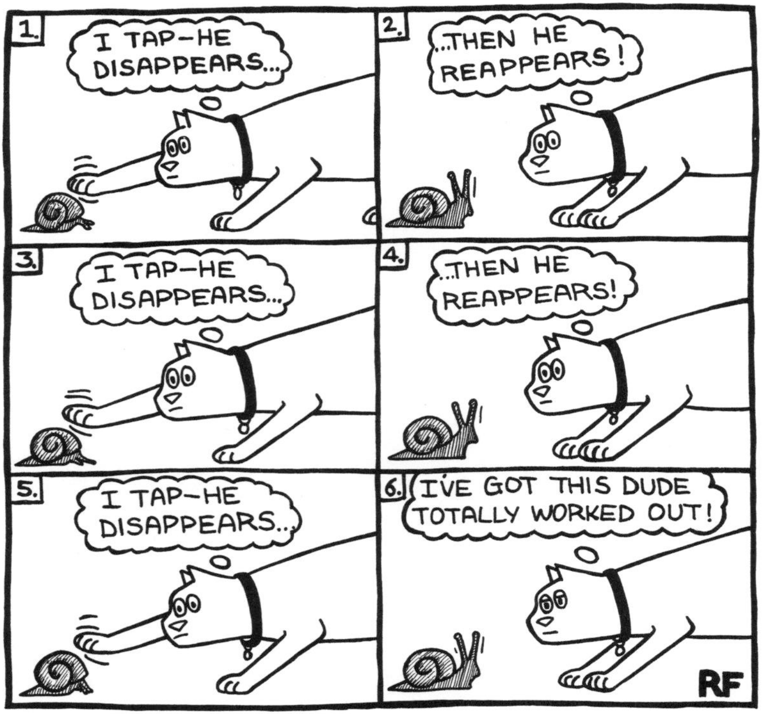
1.
I TAP—HE DISAPPEARS...
2.
...THEN HE REAPPEARS!
3.
I TAP—HE DISAPPEARS...
4.
...THEN HE REAPPEARS!
5.
I TAP—HE DISAPPEARS...
6.
I'VE GOT THIS DUDE TOTALLY WORKED OUT!
RF

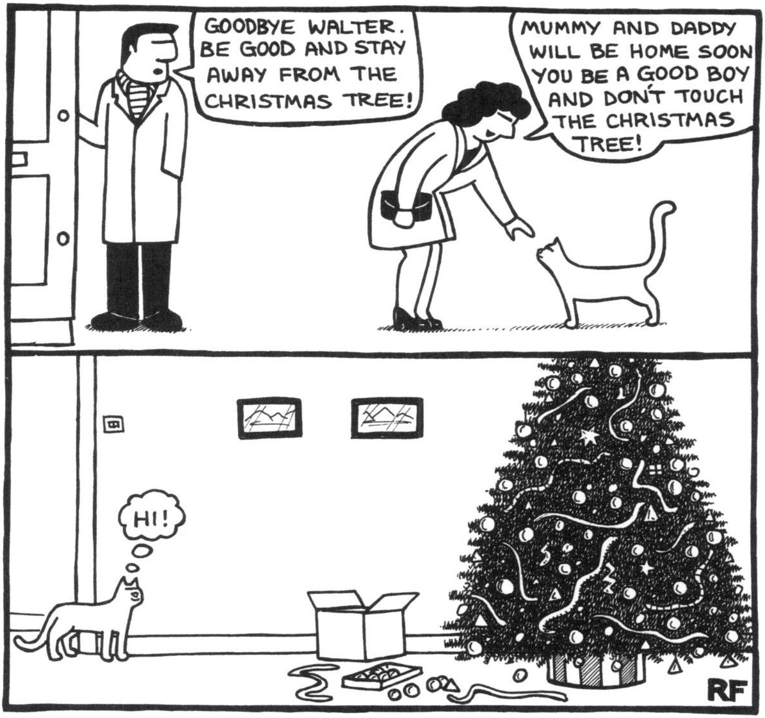
GOODBYE WALTER. BE GOOD AND STAY AWAY FROM THE CHRISTMAS TREE!
MUMMY AND DADDY WILL BE HOME SOON YOU BE A GOOD BOY AND DON'T TOUCH THE CHRISTMAS TREE!
HI!
RF

THE ATTENTION SEEKER...

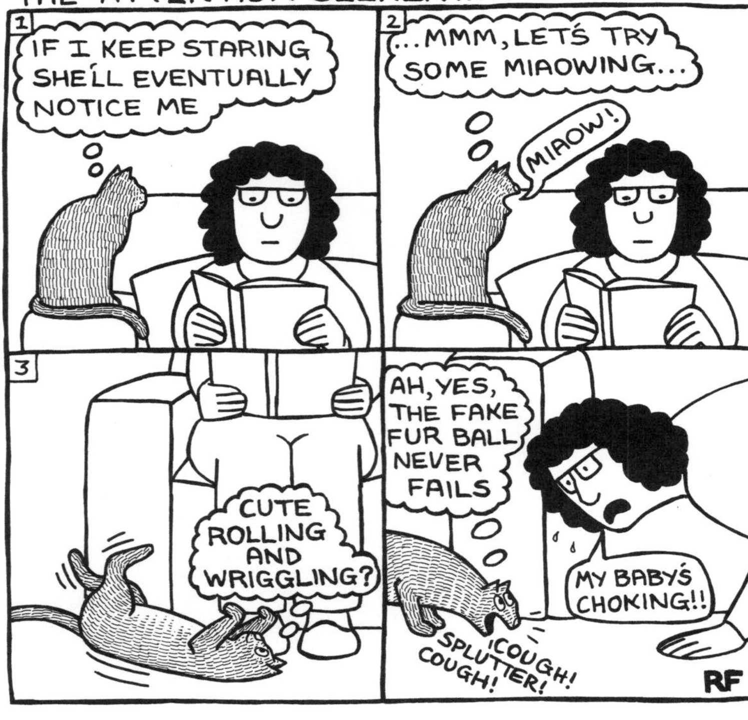

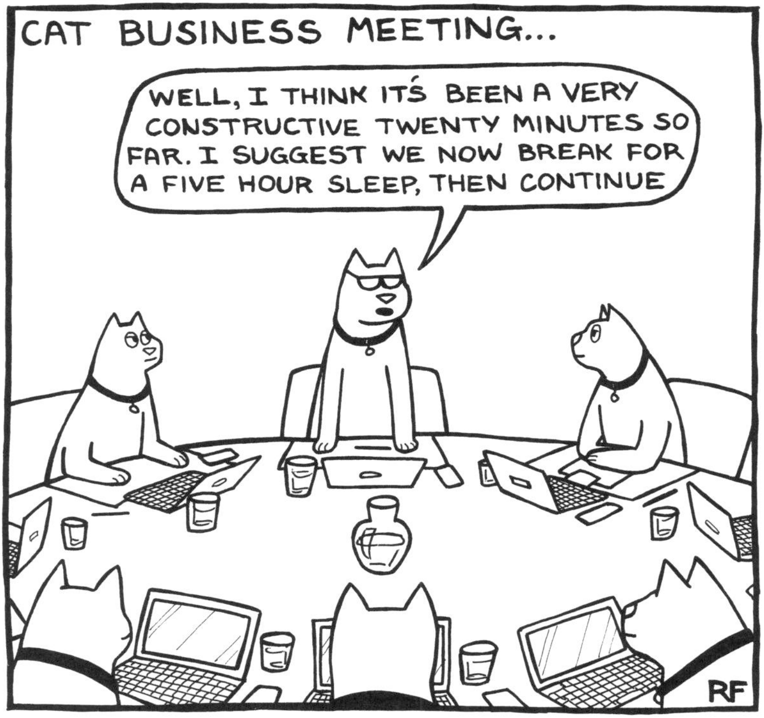
CAT BUSINESS MEETING...
WELL, I THINK IT'S BEEN A VERY CONSTRUCTIVE TWENTY MINUTES SO FAR. I SUGGEST WE NOW BREAK FOR A FIVE HOUR SLEEP, THEN CONTINUE
RF

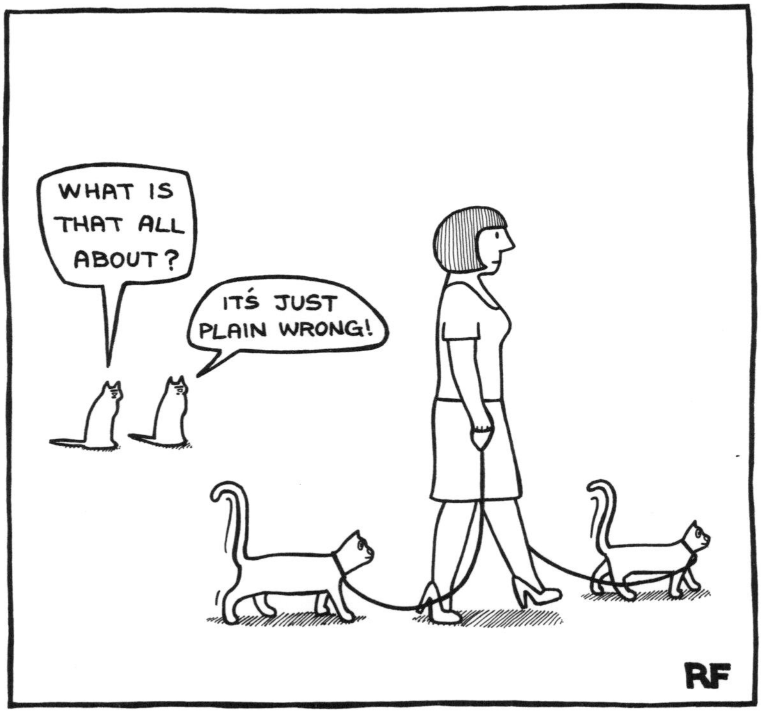
WHAT IS THAT ALL ABOUT?
IT'S JUST PLAIN WRONG!
RF

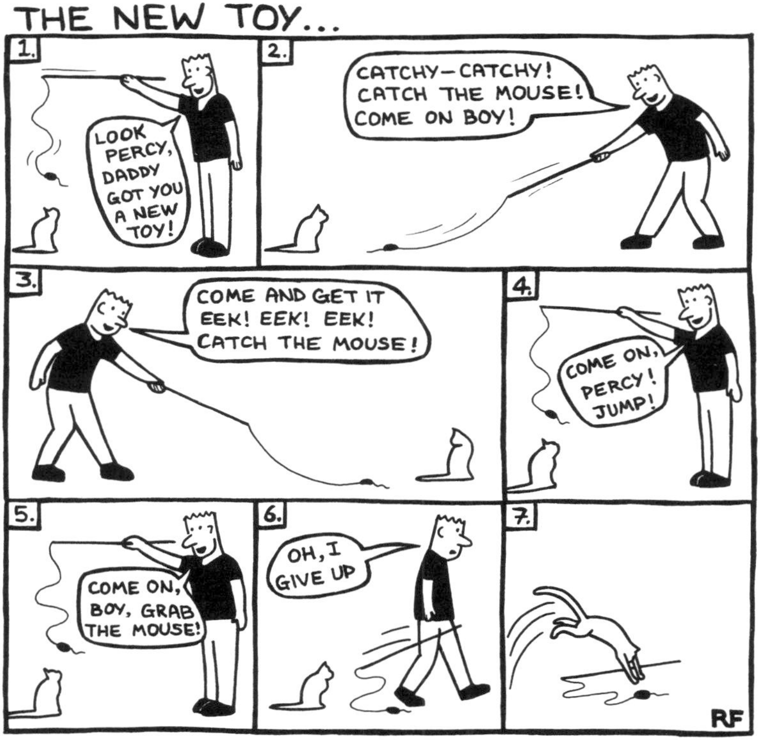
THE NEW TOY...
1.
LOOK PERCY, DADDY GOT YOU A NEW TOY!
2.
CATCHY—CATCHY! CATCH THE MOUSE! COME ON BOY!
3.
COME AND GET IT EEK! EEK! EEK! CATCH THE MOUSE!
4.
COME ON, PERCY! JUMP!
5.
COME ON, BOY, GRAB THE MOUSE!
6.
OH, I GIVE UP
7.
RF

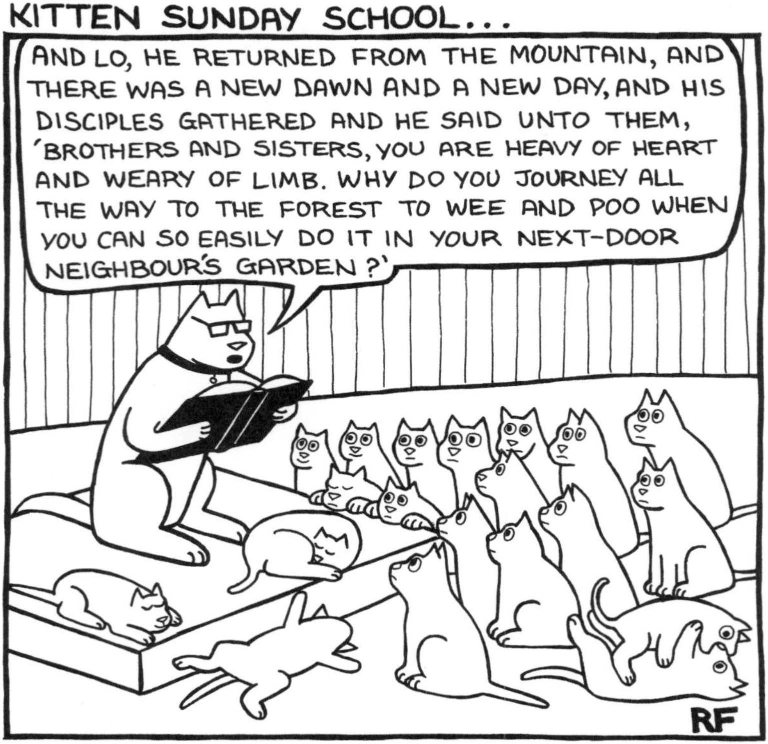
KITTEN SUNDAY SCHOOL...
AND LO, HE RETURNED FROM THE MOUNTAIN, AND THERE WAS A NEW DAWN AND A NEW DAY, AND HIS DISCIPLES GATHERED AND HE SAID UNTO THEM, 'BROTHERS AND SISTERS, YOU ARE HEAVY OF HEART AND WEARY OF LIMB. WHY DO YOU JOURNEY ALL THE WAY TO THE FOREST TO WEE AND POO WHEN YOU CAN SO EASILY DO IT IN YOUR NEXT-DOOR NEIGHBOUR'S GARDEN?'
RF

THE HEAT-SEEKING FELINE...

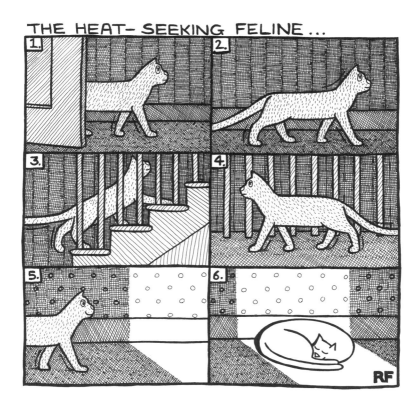

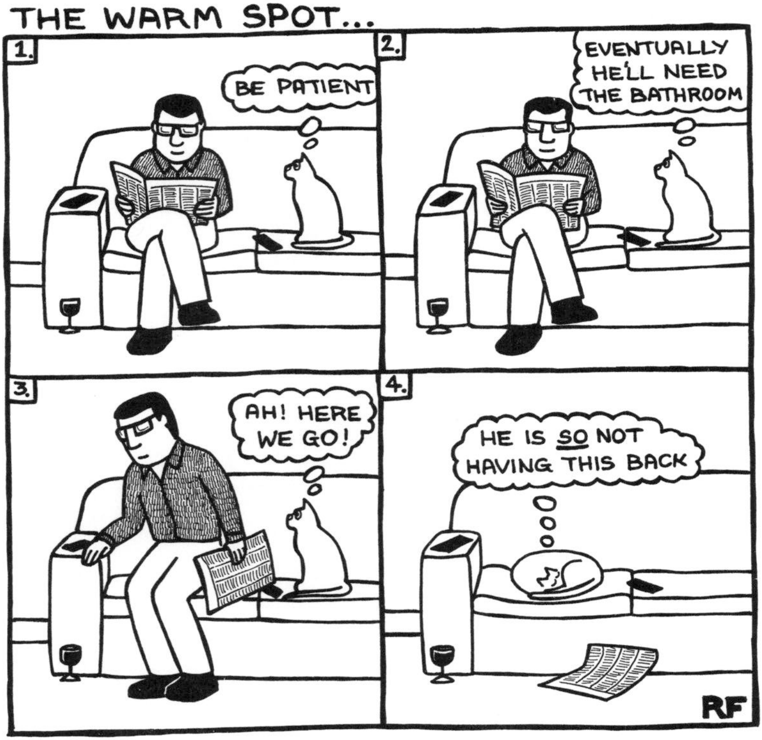
THE WARM SPOT...
1.
BE PATIENT
2.
EVENTUALLY HE'LL NEED THE BATHROOM
3.
AH! HERE WE GO!
4.
HE IS SO NOT HAVING THIS BACK
RF

1.
STRETCH,
STRETCH,
STRETCH
2.
YAWN,
YAWN,
YAWN
3.
LICK,
LICK,
LICK
4.
NIBBLE,
NIBBLE,
NIBBLE
5.
SCRATCH,
SCRATCH,
SCRATCH
I THINK THAT'S EVERYTHING ON MY 'TO DO' LIST
RF

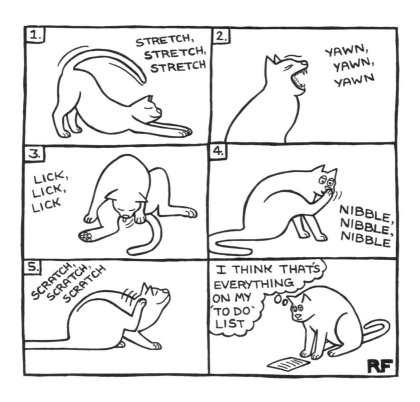

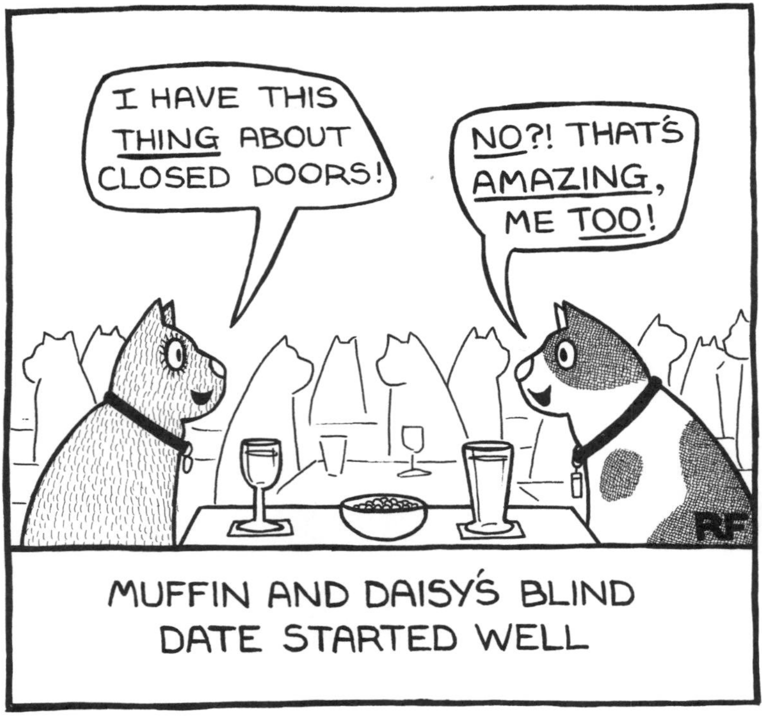
I HAVE THIS THING ABOUT CLOSED DOORS!
NO?! THAT'S AMAZING, ME TOO!

MUFFIN AND DAISY'S BLIND DATE STARTED WELL

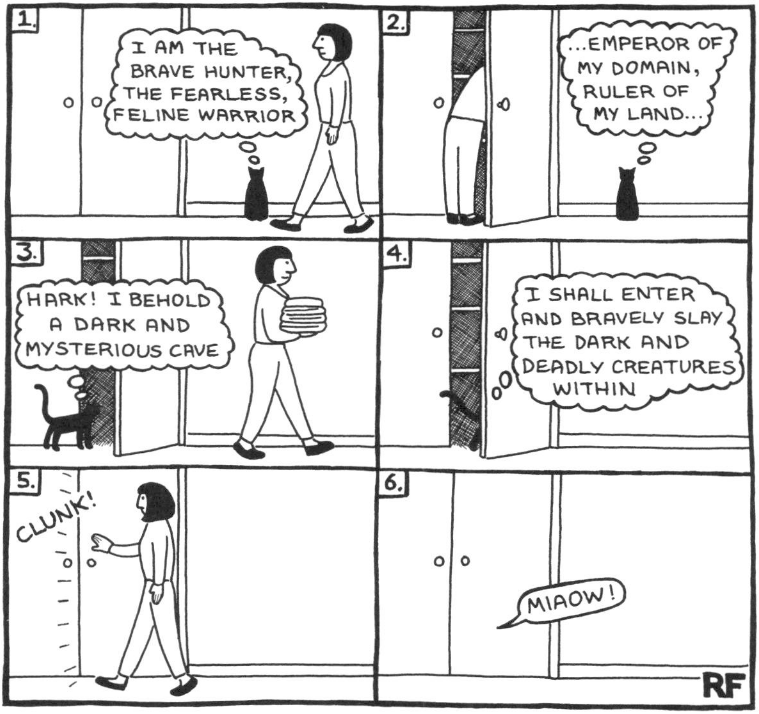
1.
I AM THE BRAVE HUNTER, THE FEARLESS, FELINE WARRIOR
2.
...EMPEROR OF MY DOMAIN, RULER OF MY LAND...
3.
HARK! I BEHOLD A DARK AND MYSTERIOUS CAVE
4.
I SHALL ENTER AND BRAVELY SLAY THE DARK AND DEADLY CREATURES WITHIN
5.
CLUNK!
6.
MIAOW!
RF

ANIMAL ELECTION TV DEBATE...
VOTE FOR ME AND I WILL BRING IN A SLEEP-LINKED TAX ALLOWANCE—THE MORE YOU SLEEP THE LESS TAX YOU PAY!
THIS DUDE IS SO GOING FOR THE CAT VOTE
PIZZA
RF

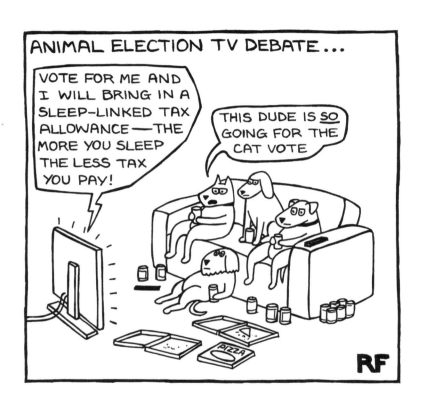

MY CLIENT PLEADS GUILTY TO THE CHARGE THAT ON 14th MAY HE STOLE A GENTLEMAN'S DARK BLUE COTTON SOCK. HE WOULD ALSO LIKE 1,478 SIMILAR OFFENCES TO BE TAKEN INTO ACCOUNT
RF

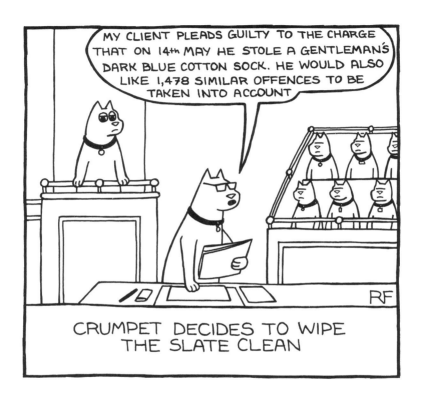

CRUMPET DECIDES TO WIPE THE SLATE CLEAN

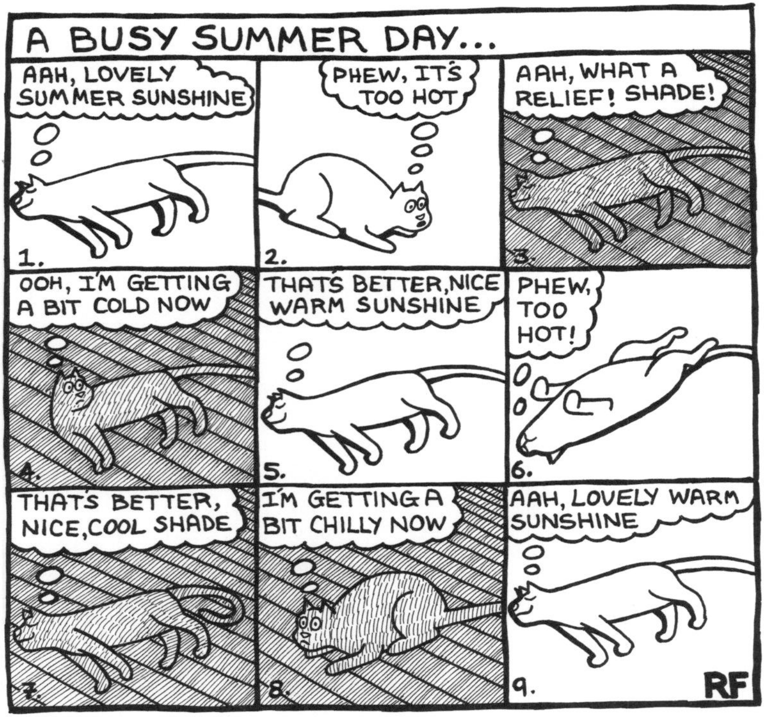
A BUSY SUMMER DAY...
AAH, LOVELY SUMMER SUNSHINE
1.
PHEW, IT'S TOO HOT
2.
AAH, WHAT A RELIEF! SHADE!
3.
OOH, I'M GETTING A BIT COLD NOW
4.
THAT'S BETTER, NICE WARM SUNSHINE
5.
PHEW, TOO HOT!
6.
THAT'S BETTER, NICE, COOL SHADE
7.
I'M GETTING A BIT CHILLY NOW
8.
AAH, LOVELY WARM SUNSHINE
9.
RF

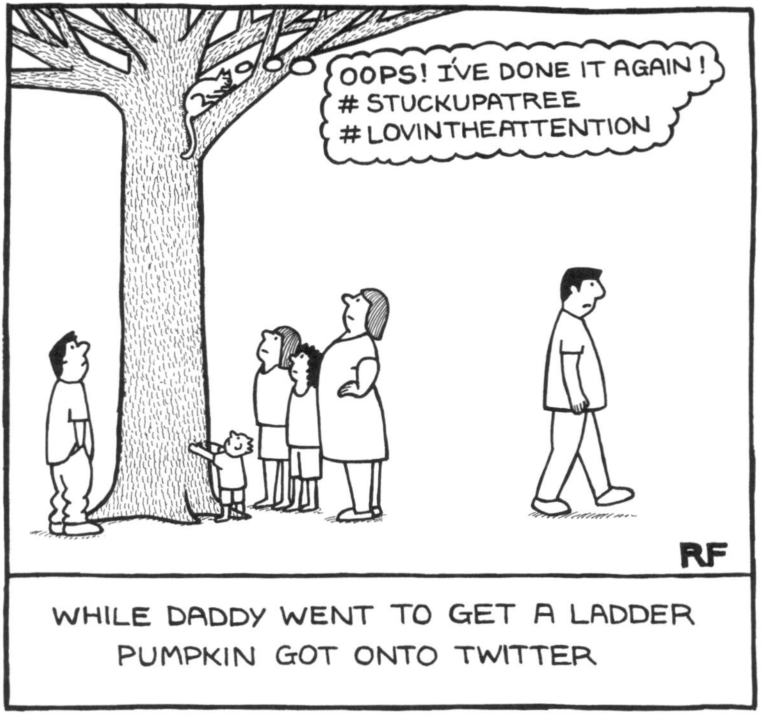
OOPS! I'VE DONE IT AGAIN!
STUCKUPATREE
LOVINTHEATTENTION
RF

WHILE DADDY WENT TO GET A LADDER
PUMPKIN GOT ONTO TWITTER

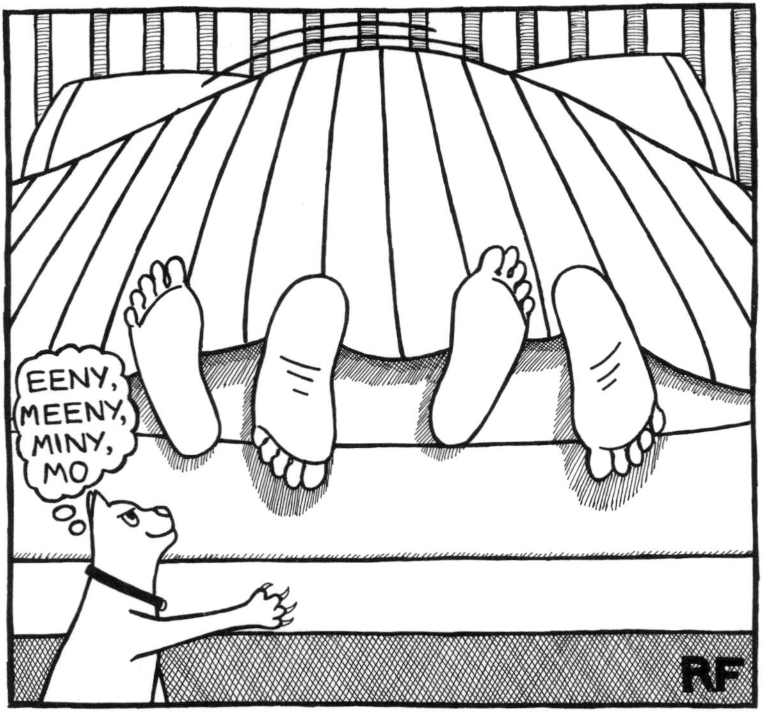
EENY, MEENY, MINY, MO
RF

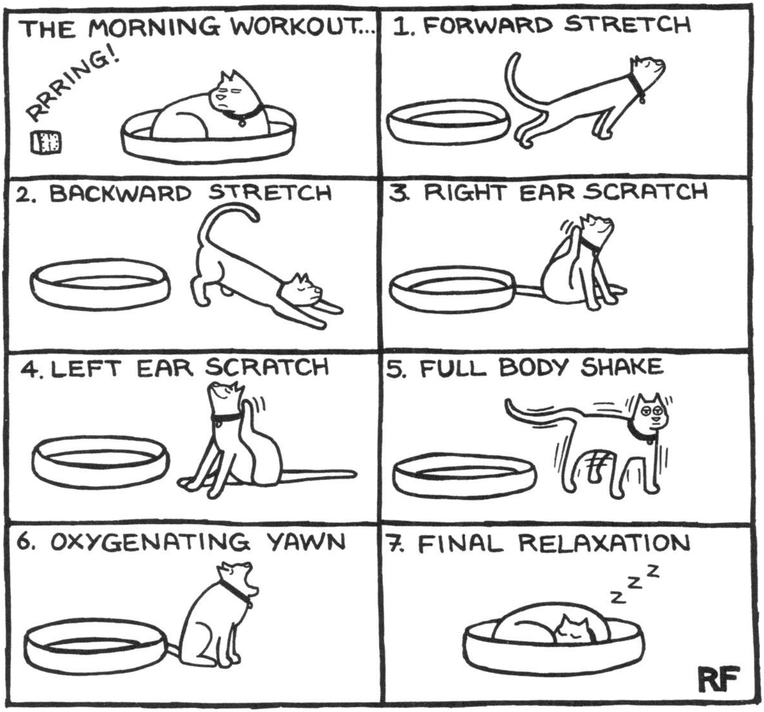
THE MORNING WORKOUT...
RRRING!
1. FORWARD STRETCH
2. BACKWARD STRETCH
3. RIGHT EAR SCRATCH
4. LEFT EAR SCRATCH
5. FULL BODY SHAKE
6. OXYGENATING YAWN
7. FINAL RELAXATION
Z Z Z
RF

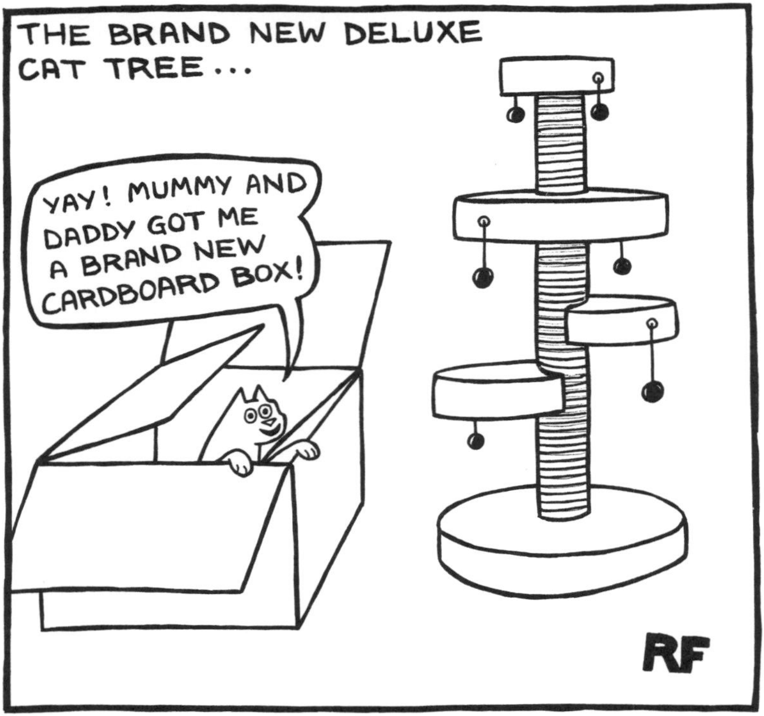
THE BRAND NEW DELUXE CAT TREE...
YAY! MUMMY AND DADDY GOT ME A BRAND NEW CARDBOARD BOX!
RF

COUPLES COUNSELLING...

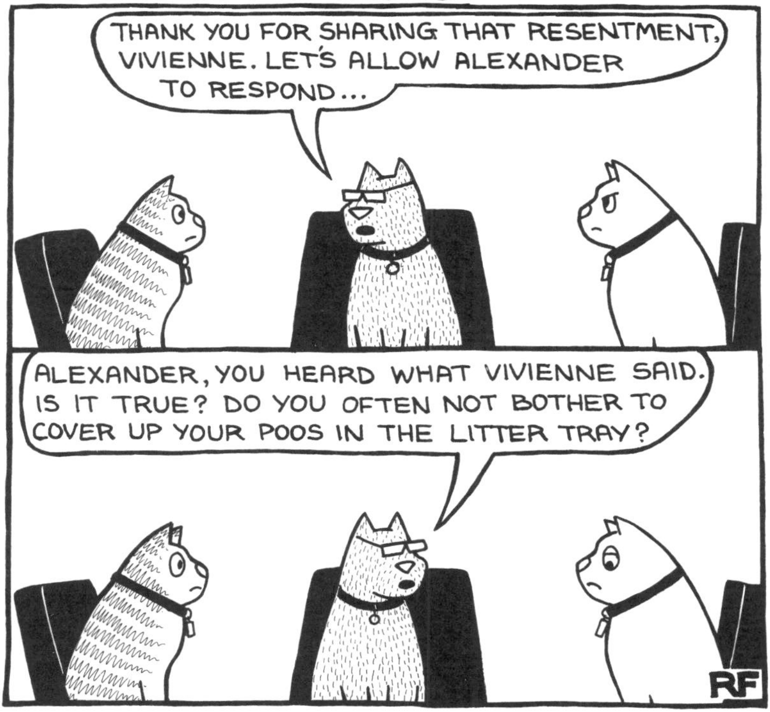
THANK YOU FOR SHARING THAT RESENTMENT, VIVIENNE. LET'S ALLOW ALEXANDER TO RESPOND...
ALEXANDER, YOU HEARD WHAT VIVIENNE SAID. IS IT TRUE? DO YOU OFTEN NOT BOTHER TO COVER UP YOUR POOS IN THE LITTER TRAY?
RF

AT THE END OF THE DAY...

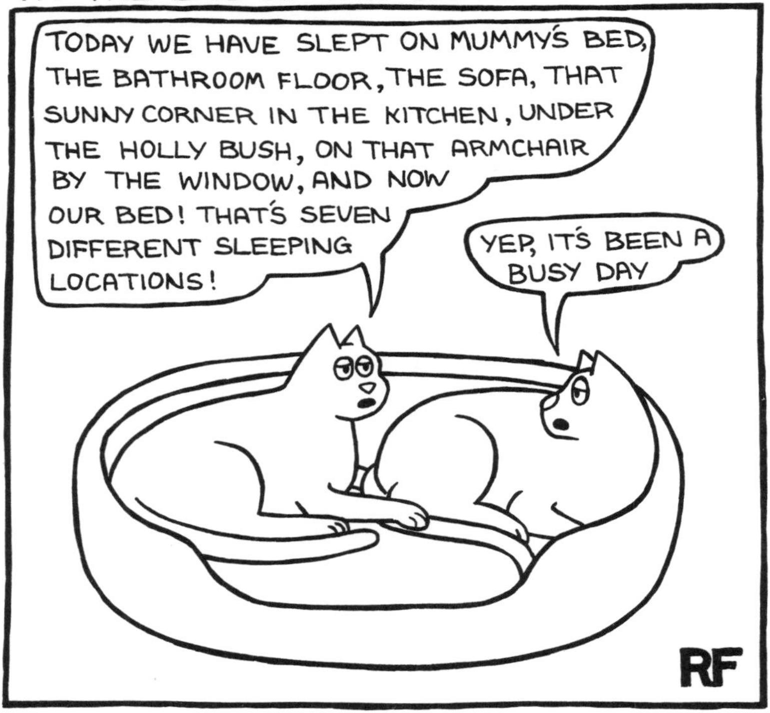
TODAY WE HAVE SLEPT ON MUMMY'S BED, THE BATHROOM FLOOR, THE SOFA, THAT SUNNY CORNER IN THE KITCHEN, UNDER THE HOLLY BUSH, ON THAT ARMCHAIR BY THE WINDOW, AND NOW OUR BED! THAT'S SEVEN DIFFERENT SLEEPING LOCATIONS!
YEP, IT'S BEEN A BUSY DAY
RF

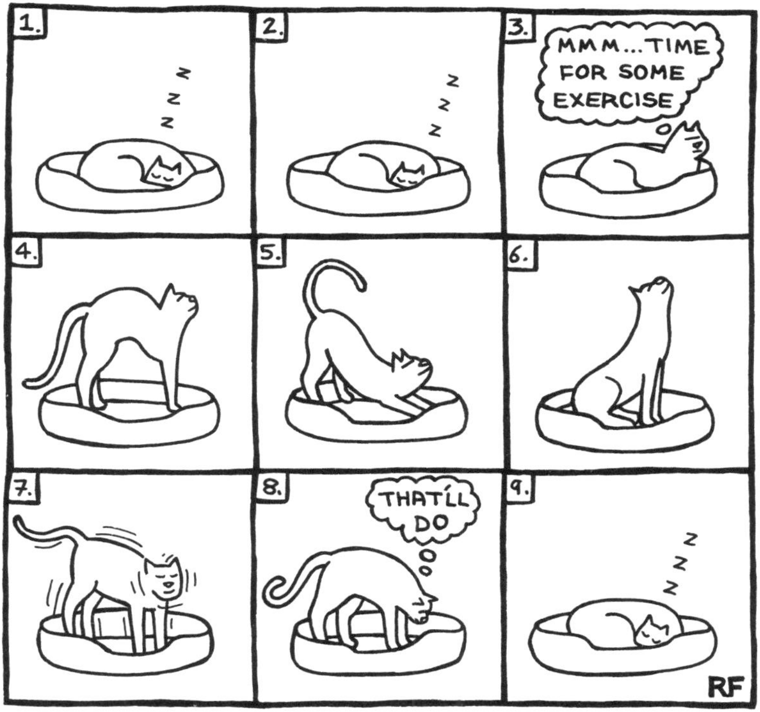
1.
Z
Z
Z
2.
Z
Z
Z
3.
MMM... TIME FOR SOME EXERCISE
4.
5.
6.
7.
8.
THAT'LL DO
9.
Z
Z
Z
RF

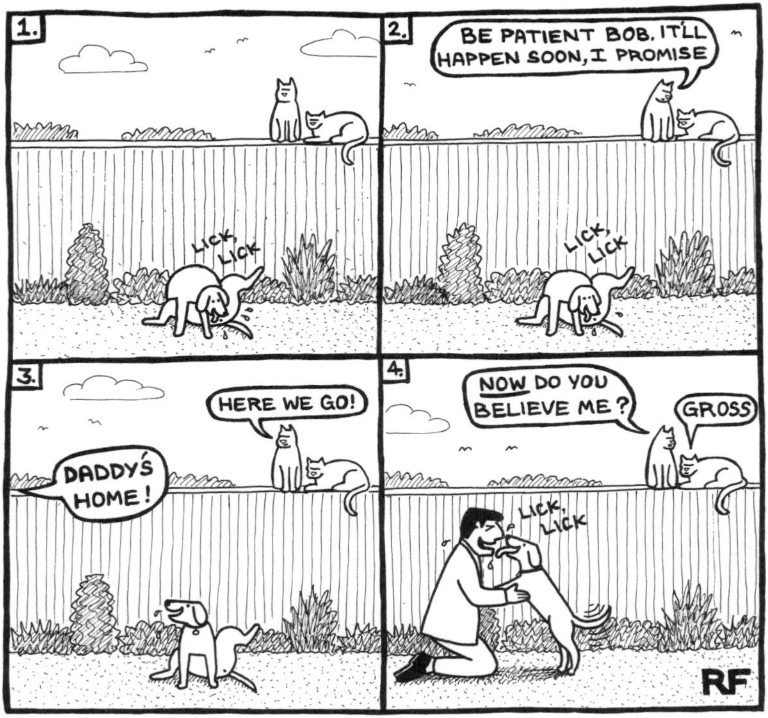
1.
LICK, LICK
2.
BE PATIENT BOB. IT'LL HAPPEN SOON, I PROMISE
LICK, LICK
3.
HERE WE GO!
DADDY'S HOME!
4.
NOW DO YOU BELIEVE ME?
GROSS
LICK, LICK
RF

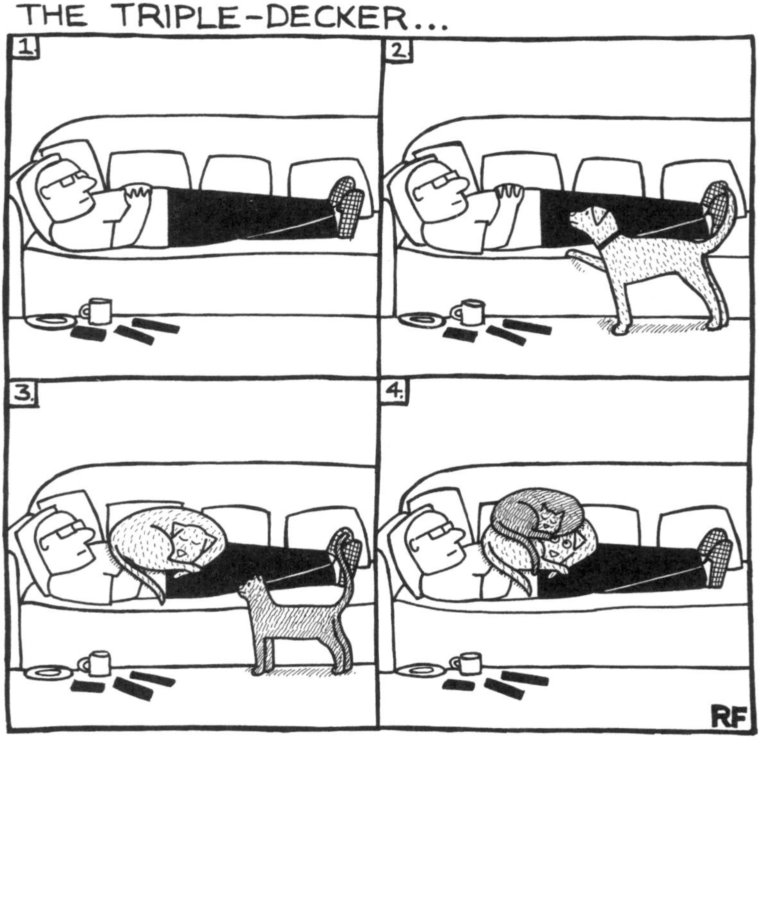
THE TRIPLE-DECKER...
1.
2.
3.
4.
RF

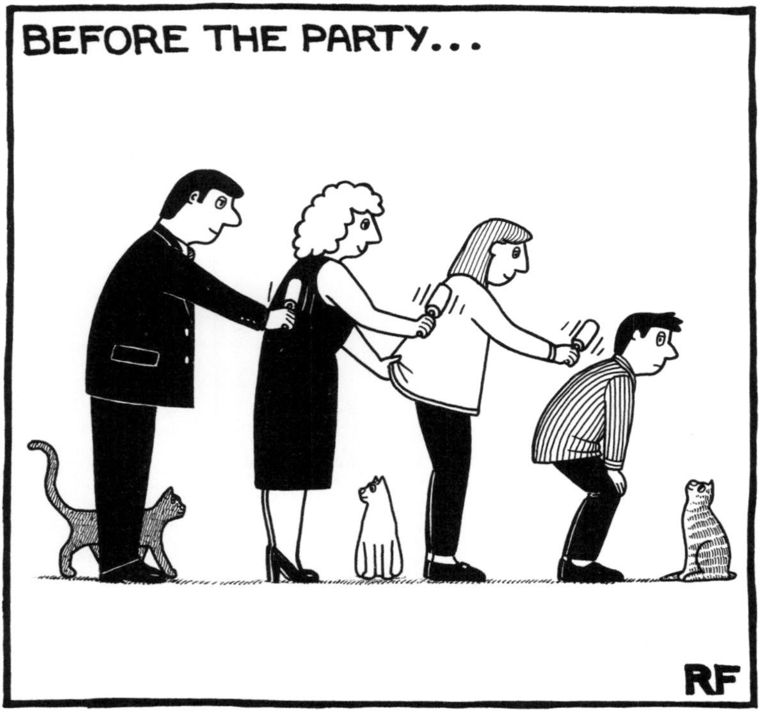
BEFORE THE PARTY...
RF

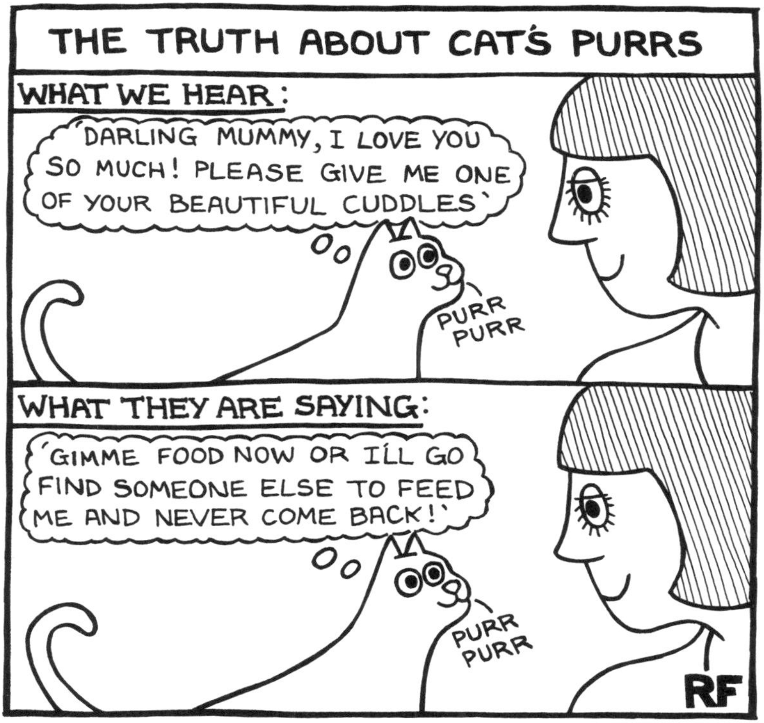
THE TRUTH ABOUT CAT'S PURRS
WHAT WE HEAR:
'DARLING MUMMY, I LOVE YOU SO MUCH! PLEASE GIVE ME ONE OF YOUR BEAUTIFUL CUDDLES'
PURR PURR
WHAT THEY ARE SAYING:
'GIMME FOOD NOW OR I'LL GO FIND SOMEONE ELSE TO FEED ME AND NEVER COME BACK!'
PURR PURR
RF

THE LITTLE HUNTER...
1.
OH, LOOK, A BIRDY IN THE SKY!
2.
COME HERE LITTLE BIRDY! LET ME CATCH YOU!
3.
COME DOWN, LET ME CATCH YOU AND EAT YOU UP!
4.
YAY, I THINK IT'S COMING! IT'S GETTING BIGGER!
5.
MUCH BIGGER!
6.
RF

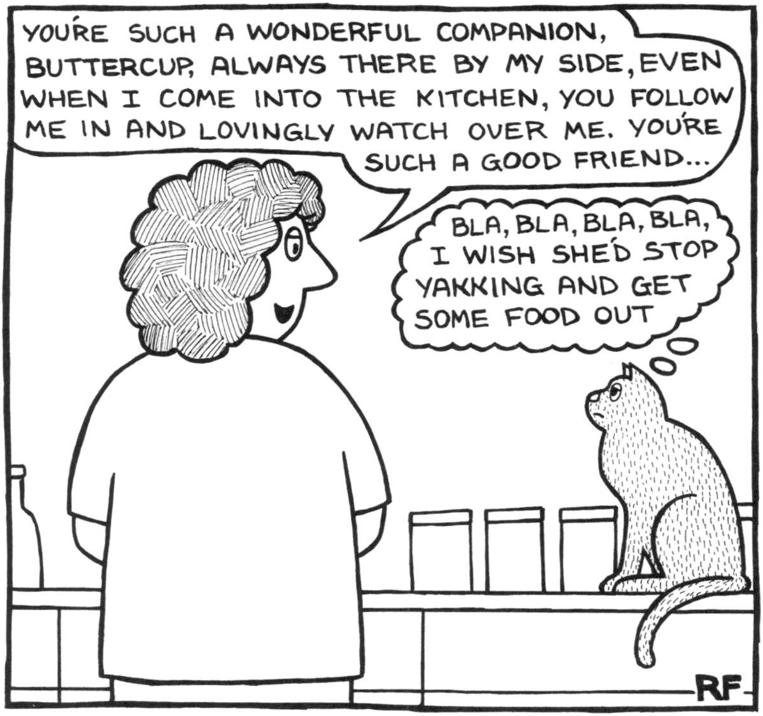
YOU'RE SUCH A WONDERFUL COMPANION, BUTTERCUP, ALWAYS THERE BY MY SIDE, EVEN WHEN I COME INTO THE KITCHEN, YOU FOLLOW ME IN AND LOVINGLY WATCH OVER ME. YOU'RE SUCH A GOOD FRIEND...
BLA, BLA, BLA, BLA, I WISH SHE'D STOP YAKKING AND GET SOME FOOD OUT
RF

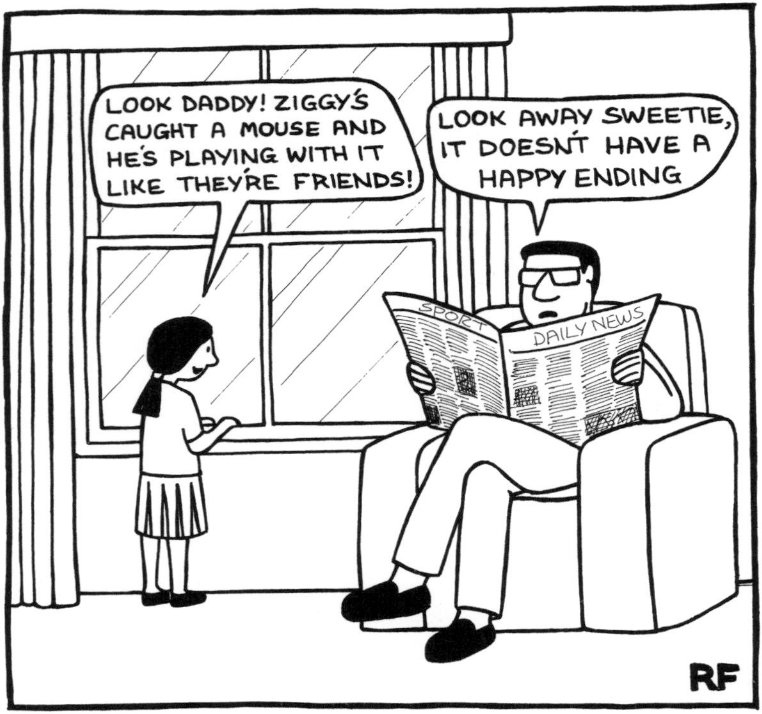
LOOK DADDY! ZIGGY'S CAUGHT A MOUSE AND HE'S PLAYING WITH IT LIKE THEY'RE FRIENDS!
LOOK AWAY SWEETIE, IT DOESN'T HAVE A HAPPY ENDING
SPORT
DAILY NEWS
RF

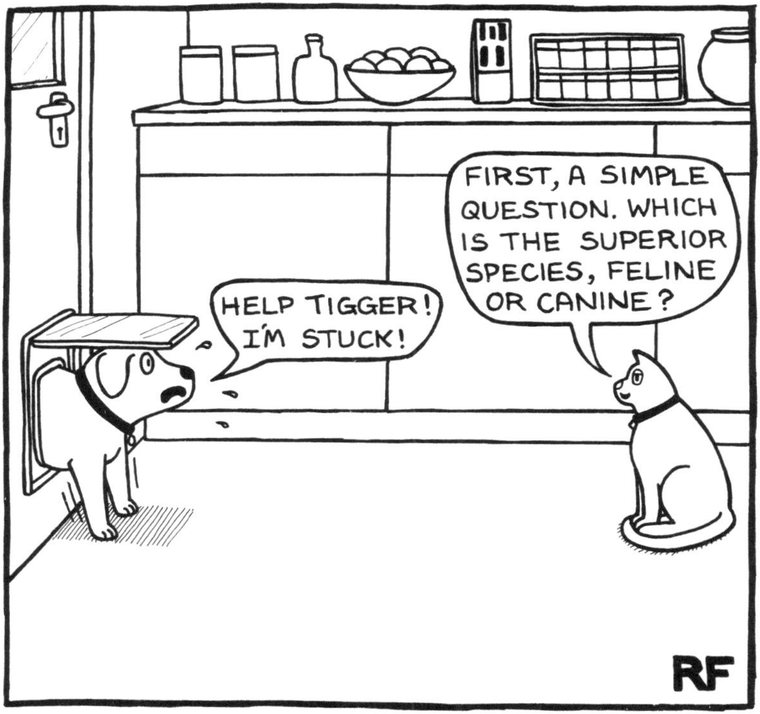
HELP TIGGER! I'M STUCK!
FIRST, A SIMPLE QUESTION. WHICH IS THE SUPERIOR SPECIES, FELINE OR CANINE?
RF

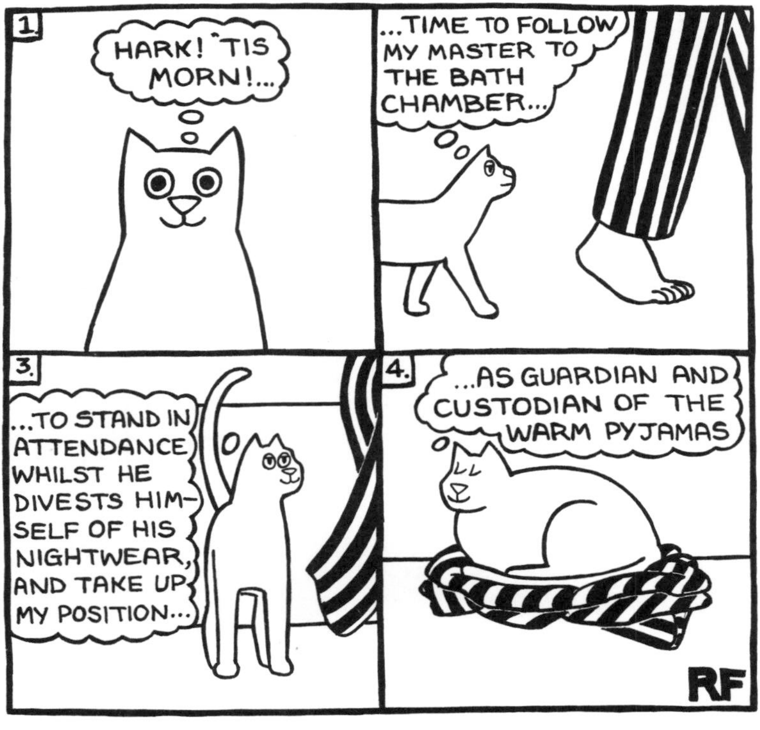
1.
HARK! 'TIS MORN!...
...TIME TO FOLLOW MY MASTER TO THE BATH CHAMBER...
3.
...TO STAND IN ATTENDANCE WHILST HE DIVESTS HIM-SELF OF HIS NIGHTWEAR, AND TAKE UP MY POSITION...
4.
...AS GUARDIAN AND CUSTODIAN OF THE WARM PYJAMAS
RF

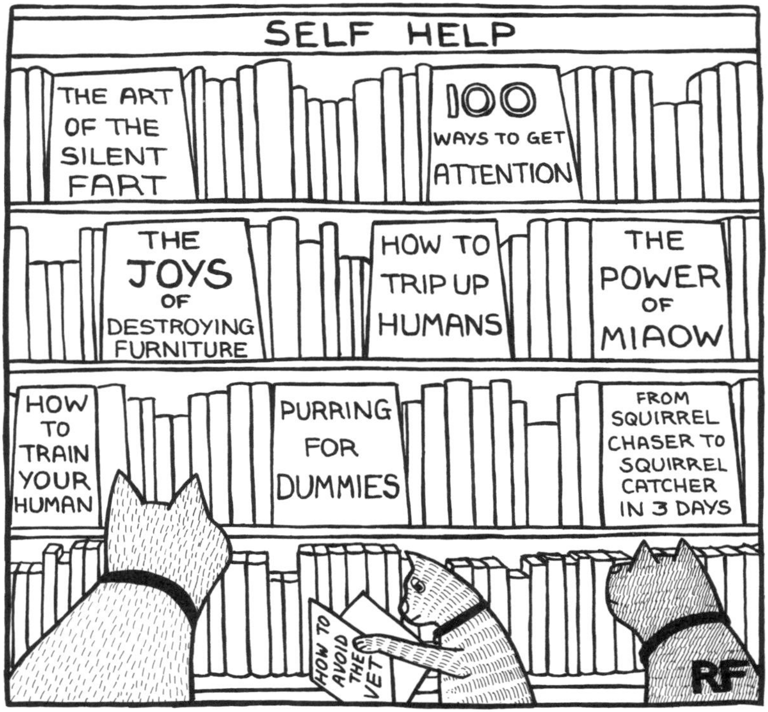
SELF HELP
THE ART OF THE SILENT FART
100 WAYS TO GET ATTENTION
THE JOYS OF DESTROYING FURNITURE
HOW TO TRIP UP HUMANS
THE POWER OF MIAOW
HOW TO TRAIN YOUR HUMAN
PURRING FOR DUMMIES
FROM SQUIRREL CHASER TO SQUIRREL CATCHER IN 3 DAYS
HOW TO AVOID THE VET
RF

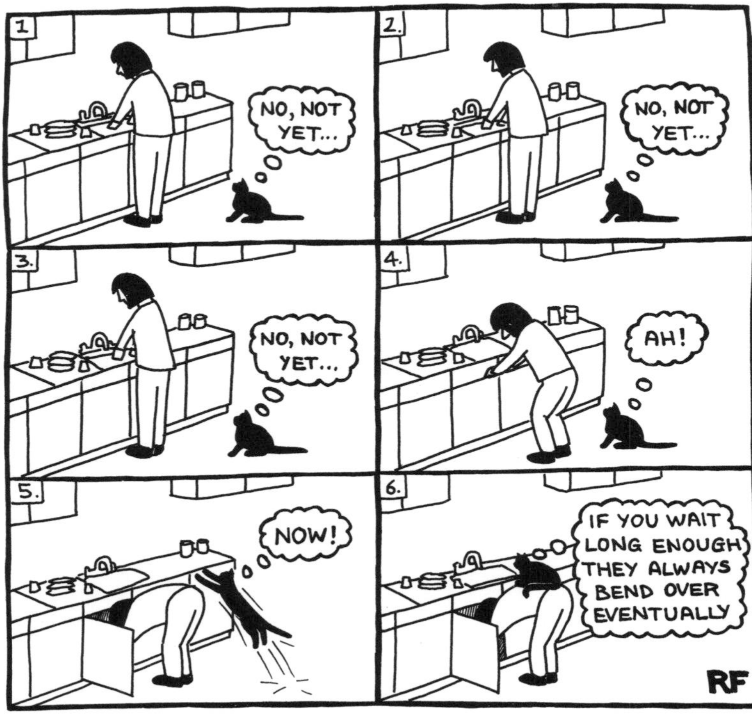
1
NO, NOT YET...
2.
NO, NOT YET...
3.
NO, NOT YET...
4.
AH!
5.
NOW!
6.
IF YOU WAIT LONG ENOUGH THEY ALWAYS BEND OVER EVENTUALLY
RF

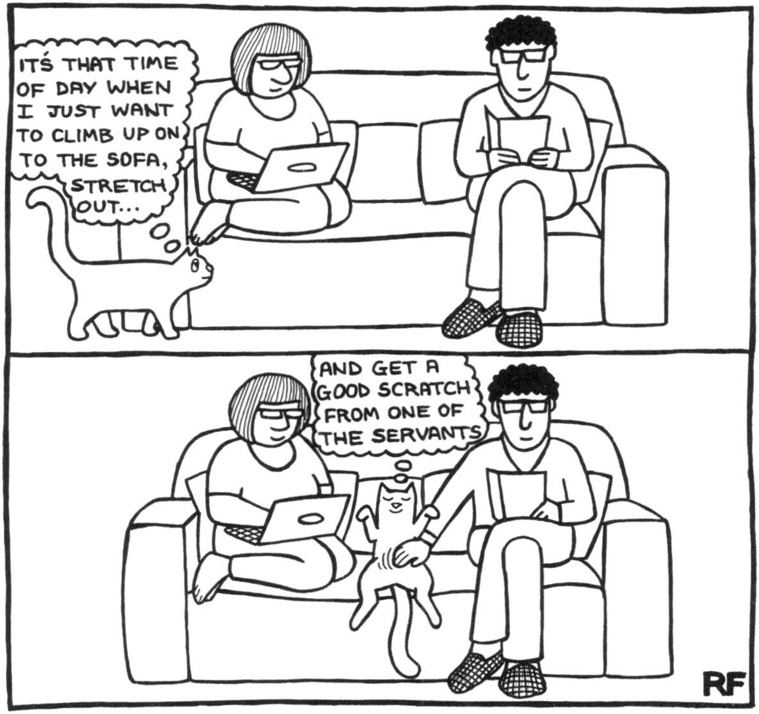
ITS THAT TIME OF DAY WHEN I JUST WANT TO CLIMB UP ON TO THE SOFA, STRETCH OUT...
AND GET A GOOD SCRATCH FROM ONE OF THE SERVANTS
RF

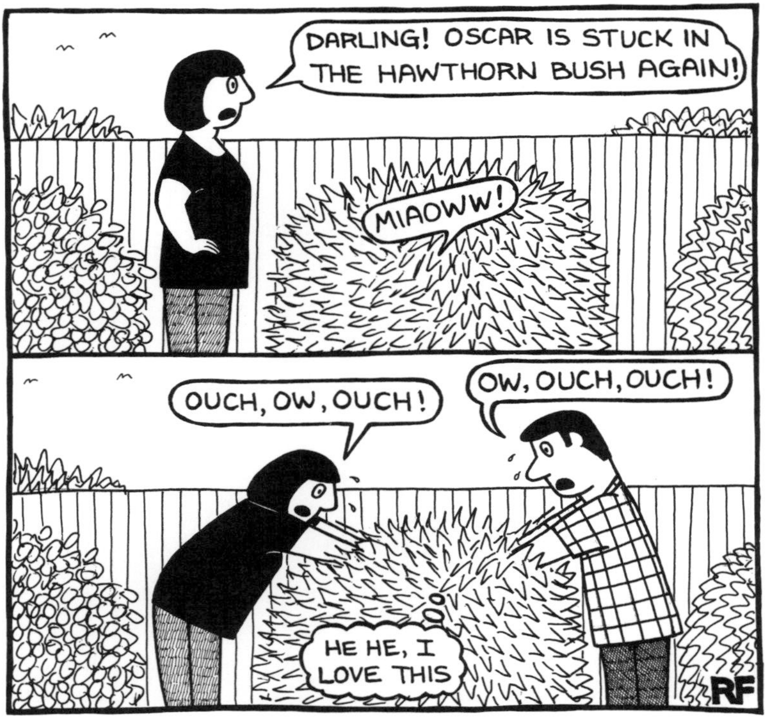
DARLING! OSCAR IS STUCK IN THE HAWTHORN BUSH AGAIN!
MIAOWW!
OUCH, OW, OUCH!
OW, OUCH, OUCH!
HE HE, I LOVE THIS
RF

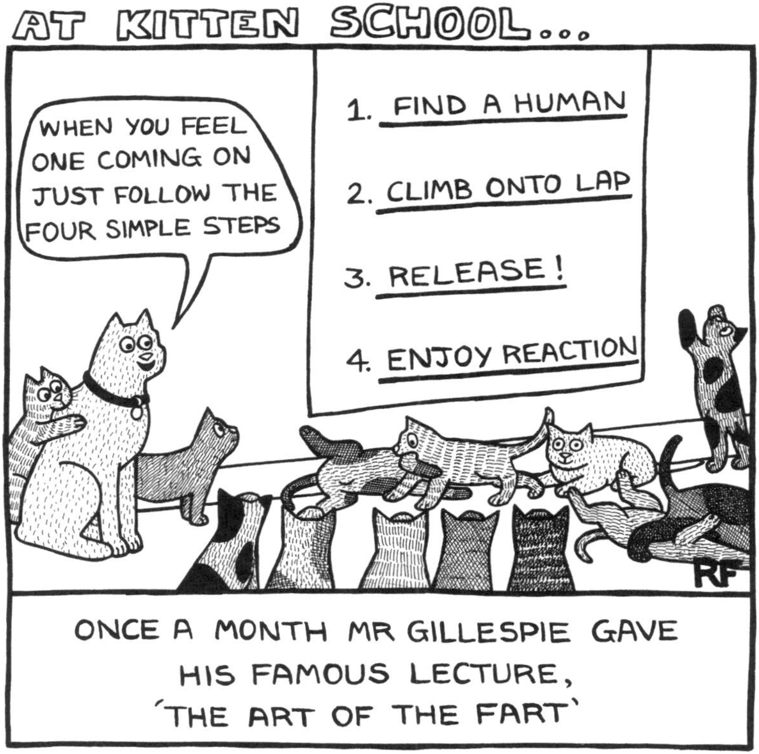
AT KITTEN SCHOOL...
WHEN YOU FEEL ONE COMING ON JUST FOLLOW THE FOUR SIMPLE STEPS
1. FIND A HUMAN
2. CLIMB ONTO LAP
3. RELEASE!
4. ENJOY REACTION
RF
ONCE A MONTH MR GILLESPIE GAVE HIS FAMOUS LECTURE, 'THE ART OF THE FART'

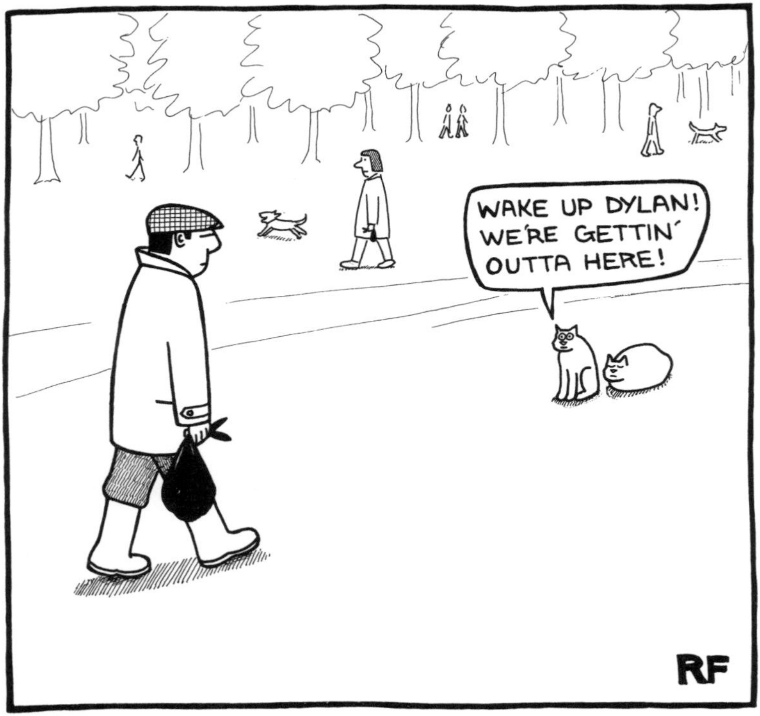
WAKE UP DYLAN! WE'RE GETTIN' OUTTA HERE!
RF

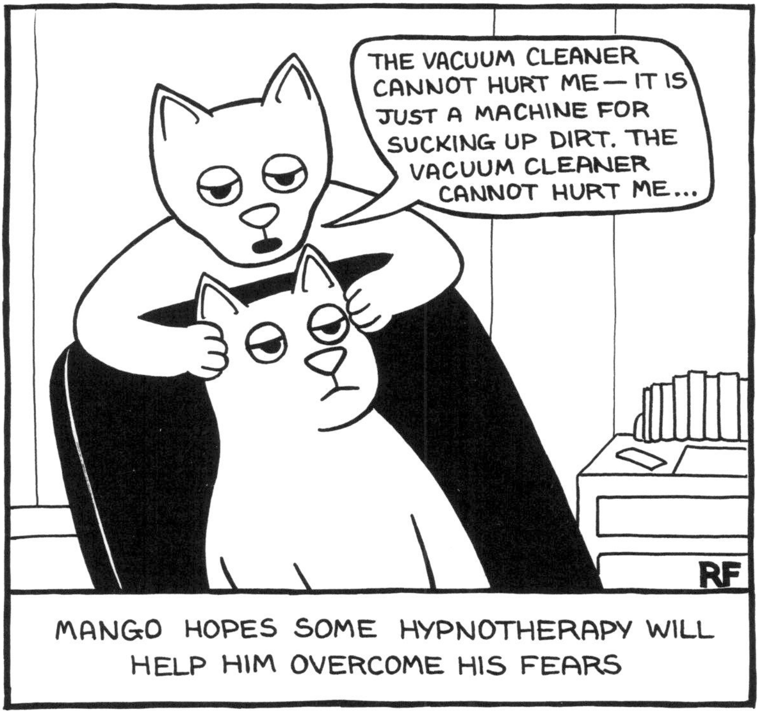
THE VACUUM CLEANER CANNOT HURT ME — IT IS JUST A MACHINE FOR SUCKING UP DIRT. THE VACUUM CLEANER CANNOT HURT ME...
RF

MANGO HOPES SOME HYPNOTHERAPY WILL HELP HIM OVERCOME HIS FEARS

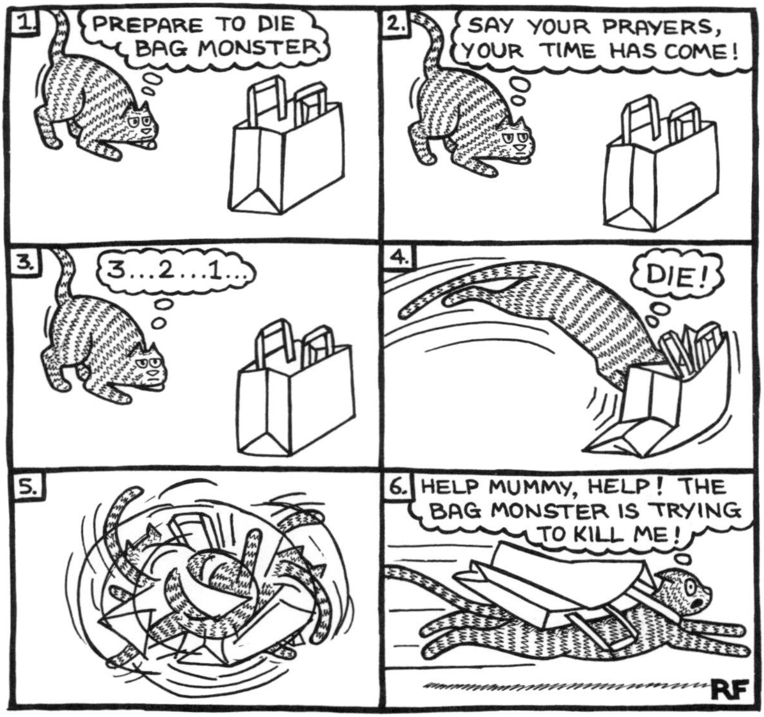
1.
PREPARE TO DIE BAG MONSTER
2.
SAY YOUR PRAYERS, YOUR TIME HAS COME!
3.
3...2...1...
4.
DIE!
5.
6.
HELP MUMMY, HELP! THE BAG MONSTER IS TRYING TO KILL ME!
RF

THE SUNBATHERS

RF

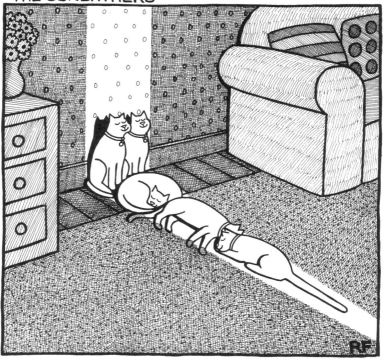

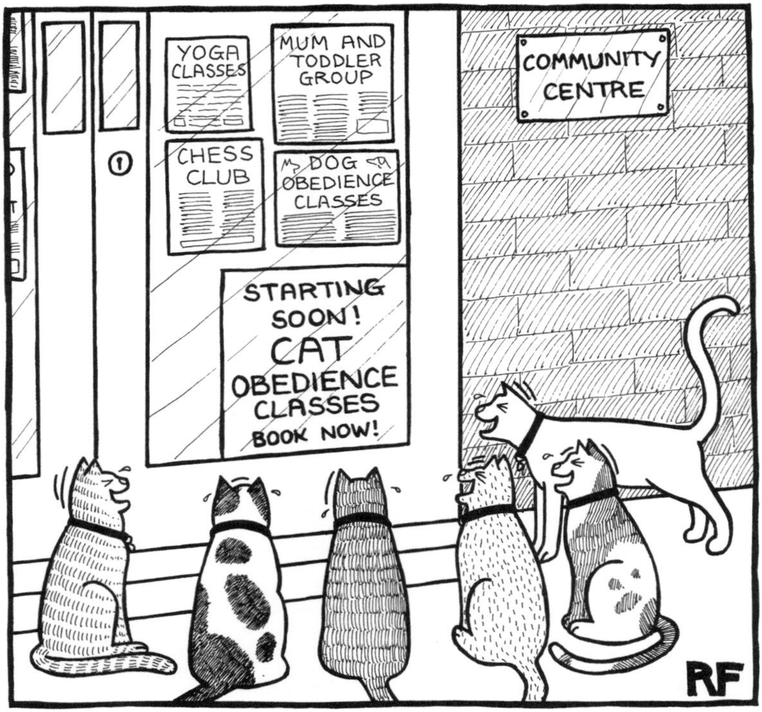
YOGA CLASSES
MUM AND TODDLER GROUP
CHESS CLUB
DOG OBEDIENCE CLASSES
STARTING SOON! CAT OBEDIENCE CLASSES BOOK NOW!
COMMUNITY CENTRE
RF

THE SEARCH...

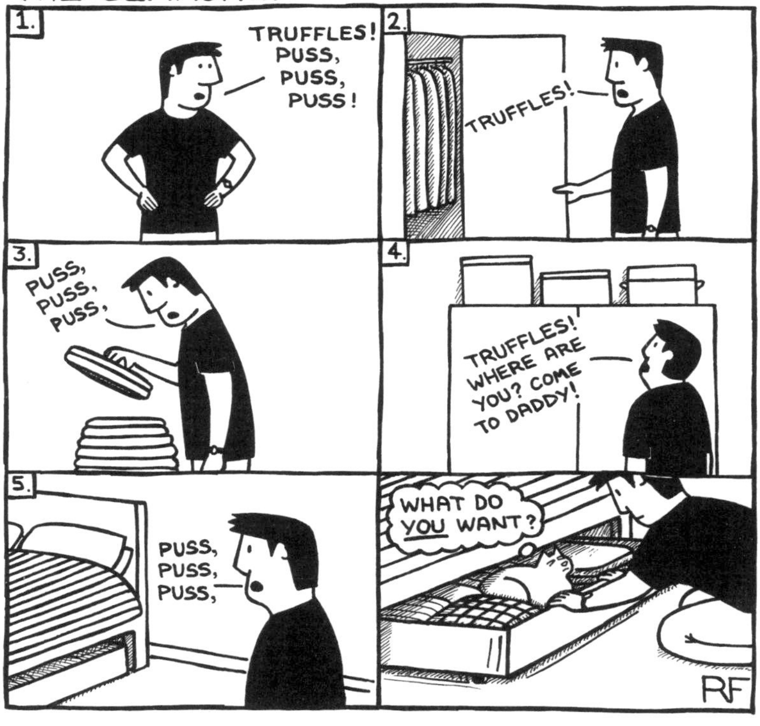
1.
TRUFFLES! PUSS, PUSS, PUSS!
2.
TRUFFLES!
3.
PUSS, PUSS, PUSS,
4.
TRUFFLES! WHERE ARE YOU? COME TO DADDY!
5.
PUSS, PUSS, PUSS,
WHAT DO YOU WANT?
RF

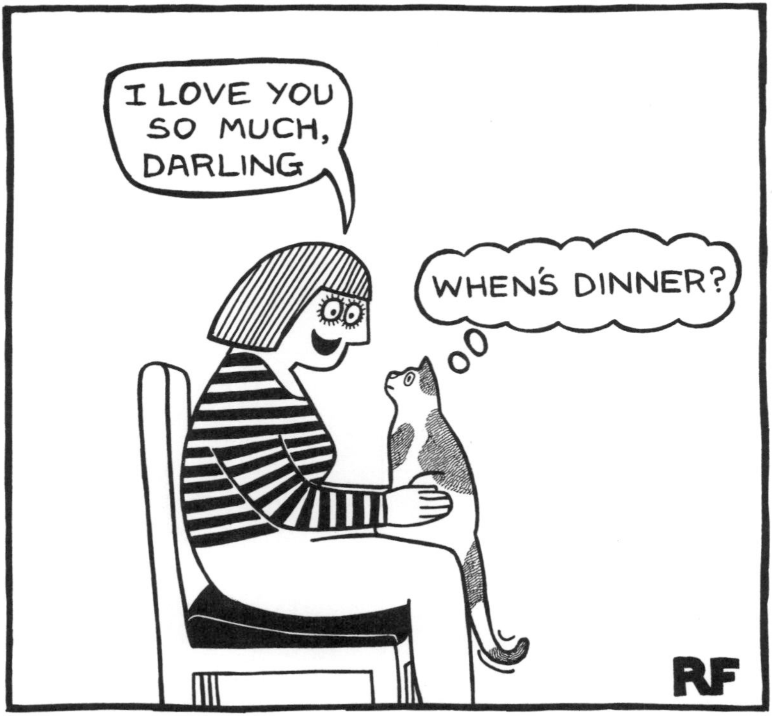
I LOVE YOU SO MUCH, DARLING
WHEN'S DINNER?
RF

THE HUNTER...
1.
3..2..1..
2.
POUNCE!
3.
4.
!
RF

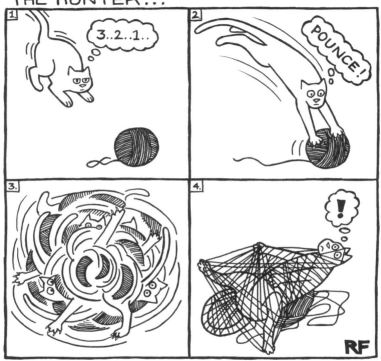

YOU KNOW YOU ARE GETTING OLD WHEN...

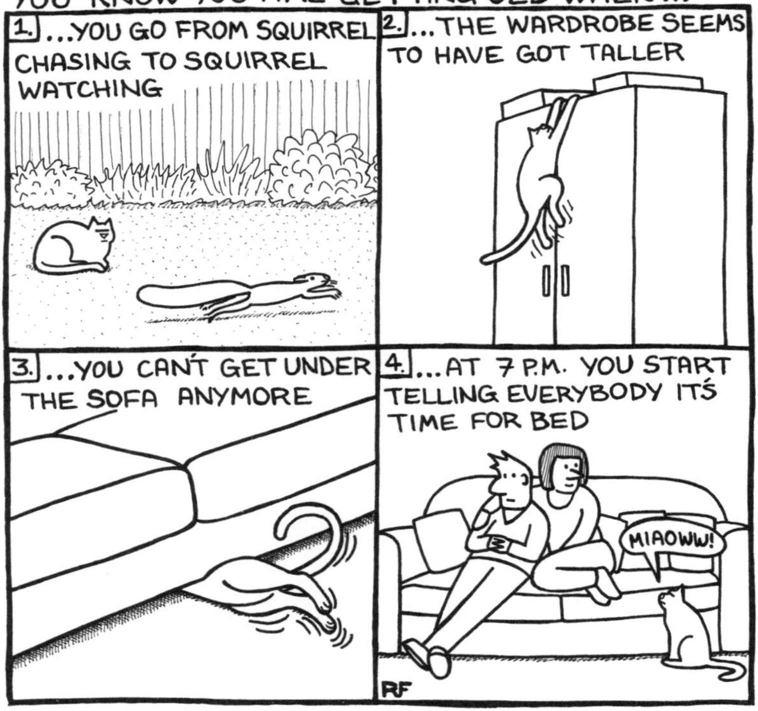
1. ...YOU GO FROM SQUIRREL CHASING TO SQUIRREL WATCHING
2. ...THE WARDROBE SEEMS TO HAVE GOT TALLER
3. ...YOU CAN'T GET UNDER THE SOFA ANYMORE
4. ...AT 7 P.M. YOU START TELLING EVERYBODY IT'S TIME FOR BED
MIAOWW!
RF

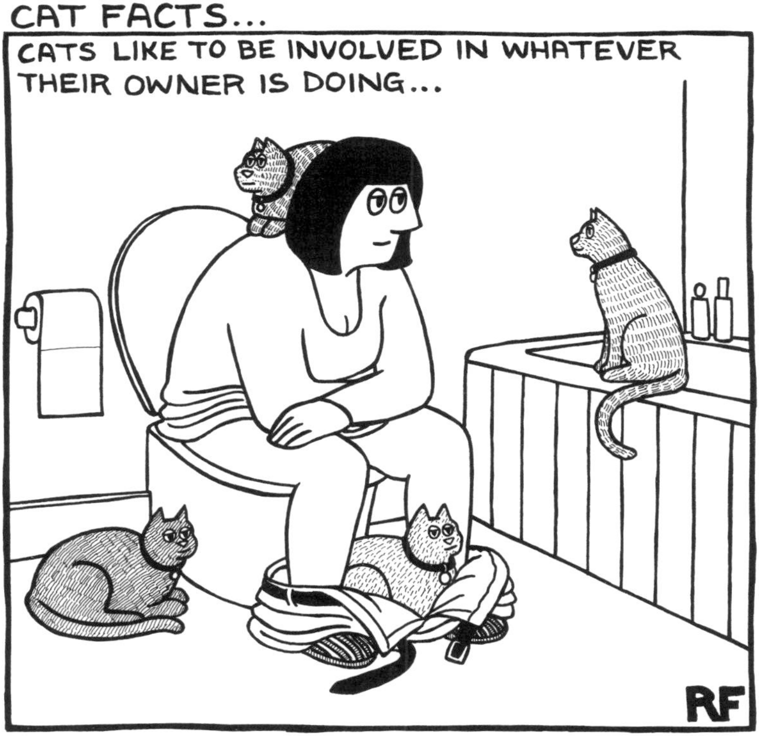
CAT FACTS...
CATS LIKE TO BE INVOLVED IN WHATEVER THEIR OWNER IS DOING...
RF

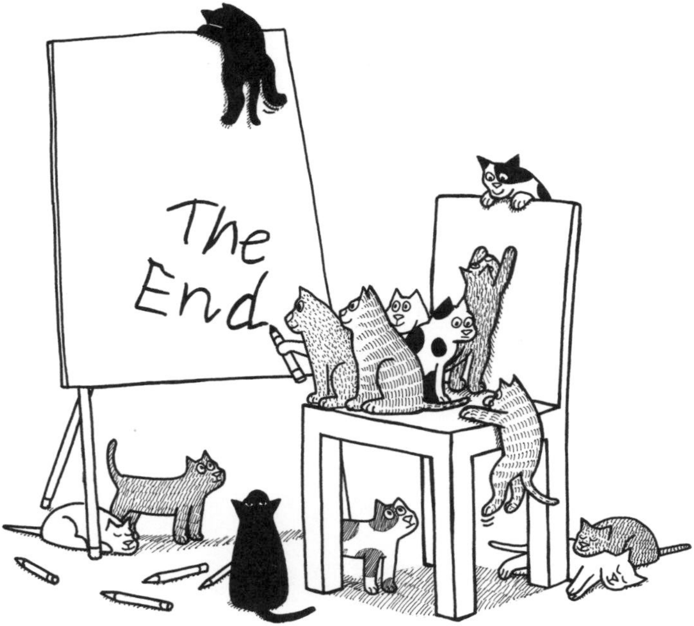
The End

About the author

Rupert Fawcett is an English cartoonist living in London. He became a professional cartoonist almost by accident when, in 1989, whilst doodling, he drew a bald man in braces and carpet slippers and called him Fred. The Fred cartoons went on to be syndicated in the *Mail on Sunday*, were published in several books and to date over 9 million Fred greetings cards have been sold in the UK, Australia and New Zealand. He is the creator of the hilarious and true to life *Off The Leash: The Secret Life of Dogs*, *Off The Leash: A Dog's Best Friend* and *Off The Leash: It's a Dog's Life*.